# MICRO FAMOUS

Become Famously Influential to the Right People

Matt Johnson

# Advanced Praise

"MicroFamous lays out the strategy to become known for a niche you own."
— Christopher Lochhead #1 Apple Podcaster | #1 Amazon Author

"Ten years from now, MicroFamous will be the new standard for building influence online. Read it now, before your competitors do."
— Dana Malstaff, CEO - Boss Mom

"I've paid thousands of dollars on coaches and seminars to pull together the wisdom that MicroFamous delivers in a powerfully clear way."
— Dr Morgan Oaks, teacher, author, speaker, podcast host

"With MicroFamous, Matt Johnson has developed a clear, concise, and ridiculously easy-to-follow roadmap to achieving microfame, the phenomenon of becoming well-known and influential to *exactly* the right people. No matter where your expertise lies, MicroFamous can help you build up a solid reputation as a thought leader – probably quicker than you think!"
— Liana Ling, Agency Owner / Lead Generation Specialist

"Regardless of what business you're in, MicroFamous not only guides you to attract ideal prospects, but to leverage resonant content effectively... and start loving your client relationships again (or maybe for the first time)."
— Kelly Campbell, Agency Transformation Coach

"Matt takes the crazy nebulous aspects of strategic influence and impact and distills them down to a clear, practical and compelling road map for those who dare accept his challenge. MicroFamous challenges each of us to step out of the shadows and dynamically share our lives with others"
— James Colburn, Business Coach & Author of RESUCCEED

"Matt knows what he is saying because he's done it himself. Wish I had this resource back when I got started. Grab a copy if you want to turn your expertise into cash."
— Lars Hedenborg, Business Coach, Founder of Real Estate B-School

"From a guy who has Narcolepsy when he reads I haven't been able to put this down. It's like you're putting into words what I've been doing yet filling in the gaps. What a gift for anyone who reads this book!"

– Hank Avink, Business Coach & Founder of National Coaching League

"Matt does a great job of breaking down what it really means to have influence and grow your brand. Once you understand why top businesses and leaders in the industry are remembered you gain clarity on how you can accomplish it yourself."
– Nate Hirsch, Founder of OutsourceSchool.com

"Matt Johnson gets it. His approach to getting known within your ideal community is spot on and deals with the exhausting yet common mistake of trying to be everything to everyone. I love the idea of being MicroFamous. Read this book. Get seen. Get noticed. Get known!"
– Todd Tramonte, Business Coach & Founder of Real Estate Growth Systems

"In MicroFamous, Matt Johnson, an experienced podcaster and podcasting coach to some of the top podcasters and micro influencers working today, lays out a compelling case. It's easy to read and very well-written. A "must have" if you want to be famous in your niche!"
– Ellen Violette, Award-winning Book Coach, Multiple #1 Bestselling Author

"If you're serious about doing the work to grow your business and are frustrated with all of the competitive noise in the marketplace, then Matt Johnson's book MicroFamous is for you. It's a thoughtful step-by-step guide to select and capture your niche that every entrepreneur should read!"

– Mark E. Green, Author of *Activators- A CEO's Guide to Clearer Thinking and Getting Things Done* and *Creating a Culture of Accountability*

"MicroFamous opened my eyes on how to truly dominate a category. Instead of trying to be seen by a massive audience, how about being famous in a smaller audience. It seems counterintuitive but makes sense....Shrinking The Battlefield expands our ability to be famous".
– Greg Harrelson, Founder – C21 The Harrelson Group

# Contents

## PART TWO: SYSTEM

## PART THREE: TACTICS

# Ready to get featured on podcasts?

**Get the Free Masterclass:**
*How to Get Podcast Hosts to*
*Feature You as an <u>Expert Thought Leader</u>...*
*Without Taking Time Away From Your Business*

We'll share the 3 story hooks that get podcast hosts to say
YES, the 4 keys to create thought leader status, and how
to start getting featured within 2 weeks.

**Register at: getmicrofamous.com/masterclass**

# Thinking of launching a podcast?

## Claim your complimentary copy of
## *The 10X ROI Podcast Checklist*

Just to say thanks for buying the book, I'd like to give you the checklist 100% FREE. A simple guide to help you launch a podcast that generates 10x return to your coaching, consulting or speaking business...without a big audience or sponsorships.

**Claim your copy at: getmicrofamous.com/10x**

# Acknowledgements

**Mentors & Friends**

First, I'd like to thank the two people who were most helpful throughout the book writing process, Dana Malstaff and Pasquale Scopelliti. There is a very short list of people I can trust completely, and you two top the list. Not only do you have my best interests at heart, but you also bring rare and valuable insight that makes everything you touch exponentially better.

Dana for your perspective, creativity and resourcefulness. Thanks to you, the ideas in the book are far more clear and compelling, and the launch was smooth, effective and successful. There is simply no one in the world I'd rather brainstorm with!

Pasquale for your strong friendship, support and guidance. You push me to raise my performance, defend my ideas, improve as a leader and fulfill my destiny. There is no one in the world with better leadership and business development material, and I'm honored to be both student and friend.

Frank Klesitz for inspiration, mentorship, strategic thinking and a unique kind of support I can't find anywhere else. Johnson PR wouldn't exist without you. Christopher Lochhead for your support during one of the toughest times of my life, and for your work on category design that heavily impacted my beliefs on marketing and new media.

And to all my clients and colleagues, especially long-time clients I'm privileged to call friends, like Jeff Cohn, Jay Campbell and Greg Harrelson. I'm extremely grateful to do great work with great people, helping you make an exponential impact in the world. It's why I'm chosen to work with business coaches and consultants for the rest of my life.

## Family

First to my dad, Kevin. The impact you've made on me is impossible to overstate. You've been a superhero, a friend, an advocate, and an example of a true leader in the mold of Apostle Paul. Out of all the things I could thank you for, the most important thing you passed on to all of your children is the relentless pursuit of truth. You set the example, by your beliefs and your actions, that it's more important to know the truth than to be comfortable or to be right.

Second, to my mom, Sarah. You provided an ideal home environment, especially in homeschooling, which allowed me to read thousands of books and explore any interest. Somehow you also allowed me to spend copious amounts of time playing musical instruments, which probably drove everyone in the family nuts.

Thanks to you both and to my sisters, Rachel and Raven. Thanks to all of you, I've never questioned the love and support of my family.

## Teams

Thanks first to Azul Terronez, CEO of Authors that lead, and to my editor Emily Chambers for helping to make the book the best it could be. A huge thank you to my amazing agency team at Pursuing Results, without all of you this book would have just stayed a bunch of words on a page. By helping coaches and consultants build their businesses, we're helping to bring life-changing, problem-solving content to people who desperately need it. That's where I get a sense of impact and fulfillment, so for your help in that mission I can't thank you enough!

# Introduction

It's easy to end up with a messy, complicated, unprofitable business.

For those of us who are driven to teach, train, and lead, it's all too common. We want to serve and impact people by solving problems, adding value, and helping people avoid pitfalls, failure, and pain. We are the next generation of thought leaders.

Yet we end up with a business that keeps us overly busy, addicted to chaos, and glued to our phones. We are burning out, spinning our wheels, trying to be everywhere and sell everything to everyone all the time.

This book is for thought leaders working to build a simple, profitable business that grows *without locking us into a business we hate.*

As emerging thought leaders, we have more than an opportunity. People are starving for leadership. The world doesn't need more business experts or entrepreneurs. The world needs more leaders.

New thought leaders are perfectly positioned to capitalize on *massive* trends in the new economy. We can serve and impact people all over the world. We can reach new groups of people who look to us for leadership.

We can build a simple, profitable business around teaching, training, and leading.

Best of all, *it can be done without....*

- spending all day on social media apps
- becoming someone we're not just to grow our business
- chasing prospects and trying to convince people to sign up
- having to negotiate, defend, and justify reasonable fees
- feeling like an imposter
- wasting time trying a bunch of different things that aren't working
- watching other thought leaders get featured on the podcasts we listen to

Yet many of us fall into the trap of putting tactics first—the daily activities that run and grow our business. When we focus on tactics without a clear strategy or system behind them, it's easy to end up with a business that drives us crazy.

We spend all day glued to our phones, creating content to attract attention. We sign up clients we aren't excited about, who require more customization and hand-holding because they're not a good fit.

Then we pull back on creating content to serve those clients, and we find ourselves with a dry pipeline. So, we start over again. Over and over the cycle goes.

There is a solution, but it starts by taking a step back. Breathe. Put the tactics aside for a moment.

That's why this book is laid out in three sections, in this order: Strategy, System, and Tactics. Because to build a simple, profitable business, it starts with a different Strategy backed by a different System.

**MicroFamous is our Strategy**—*becoming famously influential to the right people.*

Then we need a vehicle that takes us to our goal. That vehicle is a **New Media Machine**—a System for creating, publishing, and promoting content that attracts an audience, builds influence, and cultivates ideal clients over time.

Once we have these two elements in place, we can use the *Tactics* that fit our Strategy and System. The secret to building a simple, profitable thought leadership business is to become MicroFamous using the New Media Machine system.

The right people are out there starving for leadership. The people we want to teach, train and lead. The people we want to serve and impact. So there's no time to waste. Let's get started.

# PART ONE
# STRATEGY

# WIN
## THE BATTLE FOR

# ATTENTION

# Fight to Win

Every day, our people are looking for solutions to their problems.

Either consciously or not, they are always scanning for new ideas, new tactics, and new tools. They are in pain and they want it to stop.

Yet there's a big challenge.

*There is so much Noise online that our people don't know who we are or why they should work with us.*

Like it or not, we are in a Battle for Attention.

To win the Battle for Attention, it's not enough to be in the fight. **We must fight to win.**

Winning the Battle for Attention determines whose ideas spread and who makes the biggest impact.

Yet how do we win the Battle for Attention when we don't always agree on how the Battle is won?

*MicroFamous* is based on this core belief: We win the Battle for Attention when we become famously influential to a very specific group of people. Not everyone, just the people we most want to serve and impact.

The biggest winners in the Battle for Attention are those who come to mind first for solving a problem. They aren't just in the conversation; they come to mind *first*.

*In fact, they become known for one thing.*

Want to become a better leader? Pick up a John Maxwell book.

Want instant transformation and motivation? Go to a Tony Robbins event.

Want to hustle your way to success through social media? Follow Gary Vaynerchuk.

Each of them is winning the Battle for Attention because they've become known for one thing.

They've been talking about one thing for so long that they come to mind first for that one thing in the minds of the people they want to serve and impact.

They have become famously influential.

And any thought leader can do the same.

So how do we fight to win?

Let's start with the basics—the elements of the Battle.

The first element is the **Audience**, a group of people who invest their attention in our content. Our Audience can include everyone from potential clients and prospects to followers and raving fans, but the heart of our Audience are the ideal clients—the like-minded people we want to serve and impact.

The second element is our **Weapons**, the new media content we use to reach our Audience. When we create content, we have officially picked up our weapons and entered the Battle for Attention.

The third element is our **Opponents**, the thought leaders and influencers trying to serve the same group of like-minded people. They probably have different beliefs or different values, or they offer a competing service. We see their social media posts; we screenshot their ads; we keep an eye on their launches.

Yet we all have a common opponent—**Noise**.

As soon as we enter the Battle for Attention, we confront the Noise—all the voices of other thought leaders, influencers, and brands trying to attract attention. We can all agree that to *win* the Battle for Attention, we must cut through the Noise.

Here's the challenge for those of us who want to teach, train and lead people.

**Attention is not enough.** Yes, we need to cut through the Noise, but in a very specific way.

**We must cut through the Noise in a way that converts attention into real *influence*. Influence that creates demand for our service. Influence that compels action. Influence that creates real sales, real clients, and real impact.**

If we cut through the Noise *without* building real influence, our business won't grow. We'll have plenty of attention, but few sales.

That's where many of us get stuck.

We spend so much time chasing attention that we fail to build real influence and demand for our service. We have eyeballs and encouragement, but no action. As a result, we don't get to serve as many clients and we don't get to make a big impact in the world.

So what holds us back from fighting to win?

It goes back to our beliefs about the Battle for Attention. These beliefs often manifest themselves in the form of questions. Questions that are based on limiting beliefs that ultimately hold us back.

We'll deal here with just three of those questions.

*Limiting Question #1. What can I do today to reach more people and attract more clients?*

When it comes to building influence and attracting ideal clients, most of us live day to day. We think if we can generate a big enough flurry of activity *today*, we can attract new clients and grow our business. We're always looking for the latest tools, tactics, or techniques to get more eyeballs on our content.

We think we're being strategic, when we're really just being *opportunistic*. We're focusing on flurries of activity that capitalize on short-term opportunities.

But there are certain outcomes that only come from consistent action over time. Real influence is one of them. The elements of real influence—Authority, Visibility, and Relationships—don't come overnight to anyone.

The more opportunistic we are, the less focus we have left for the consistent action that delivers huge, compounding results over time. Worse yet, the less focus we have for leading our Audience—the reason we started a thought leader business in the first place.

Every flurry of activity comes with a price, because they often prevent us from building systems that would solve problems once and for all.

Now let's look at the second question.

*Limiting Question #2: How can I appeal to the widest possible audience?*

This question limits us because it sets a goal based on what *we* want, not what's best for our ideal clients, who want a solution tailored for them.

As a result of this question, most of us can't explain—in one to two sentences—what we do for clients and what makes us unique. Our quest to serve *everyone* limits our ability to attract *anyone*.

We may have an amazing service based on real expertise, yet we can't express that expertise with a Clear & Compelling Idea that grabs the attention of our ideal clients.

As a result, business growth comes mainly through personal relationships, networking, referrals, and speaking gigs with a captive audience. When we tell people what we do, we get polite reactions and encouragement, but everything in our business feels sluggish.

Let's close out with the third question.

*Limiting Question #3: How can I get the most eyeballs on my content?*

This focus on top-line numbers—downloads, views, and likes—leads us away from polarizing ideas. Yet polarizing ideas are what it takes to cut through the Noise and attract ideal clients.

A quest for top-line numbers often leads us to dilute ourselves and our message, losing the very elements that make us unique and compelling. If our goal is win the Battle for Attention, we have to reach the *right* people—not just more people.

Yet there's good news. The Battle for Attention never ends. Winning and losing are both temporary. The big winners today might be runners-up tomorrow.

If we've been asking ourselves the wrong questions and chasing short-term opportunities, and we don't come to mind *first* in the minds of the right people, we can change all that starting right now.

It's never too late to start attracting an audience, building influence, and becoming famously influential to the right people.

It all starts with one decision. The decision that if we're in the Battle for Attention, we're going to Fight to Win.

# Choose a Winning Strategy

Ten years ago, publishing a video or launching a podcast was hard. Today we can do both from our smartphones.

Tools and tactics have also become insanely cheap. The additional cost of a piece of content or a follower on social media is basically zero.

As everyone gets better at tactics, it gets harder to find an edge. Any thought leader can have a podcast, a book, a website, and a social media profile.

When we find a slight advantage from tools and tactics, it rarely lasts long. Even if we build a reputation for being on the cutting edge, we've locked ourselves into a never-ending quest for the latest tweak or growth hack.

That's what happens when everyone is focused on tools and tactics.

That's just the surface world of the Battle for Attention. Anyone can be in the Battle using the tools and tactics of new media.

Strategy determines who WINS.

In the world of thought leaders, we see two very different strategies being used to win the Battle.

Some thought leaders say something so surprising, so compelling, and so polarizing that it immediately cuts through the NOISE.

Because their ideas are surprising and polarizing, those ideas spread quickly and easily. As more people resonate with their ideas, more people seek them out and share their ideas with other like-minded people.

I call this the Simon Sinek Strategy.

Other thought leaders say something less compelling, yet they say it so frequently and so consistently that they break through the Noise by sheer volume. They build an audience and a sense of momentum by simply showing up more often than their competitors.

I call this the Gary Vaynerchuk Strategy.

This strategy is where most thought leaders default. When our ideas don't cut through the Noise, we try to make up for it with volume. That just adds to the Noise.

Yet an idea that cuts through the Noise, delivered *systematically*, attracts an audience of the right people, builds influence, and cultivates ideal clients over time.

That's how we become famously influential to the right people. That's the MicroFamous strategy.

# Cut through the

NOISE

## WITH A CLEAR AND
## COMPELLING IDEA

# Cut Through the Noise
# With a Clear & Compelling Idea

Every business is based on an idea.

The companies we admire most are based on ideas we admire. Ideas we believe in. Ideas we want to support and champion.

Everything should be available for sale online (Amazon)

All cars should be electric (Tesla)

Shaving should be simple and inexpensive (Dollar Shave Club)

Technology should be simple, cool, and easy to use (Apple)

At the heart of those businesses lives a Clear & Compelling Idea, often a guiding principle or a vision of how the world should be. A north star that guides the company and its products.

Looking to follow in the footsteps of these admired companies, business leaders set out in search of an idea of their own. An idea that can attract customers and fuel growth and expansion.

Typically, the search goes off the rails immediately.

They begin the search by looking for an idea that serves as an umbrella. A big, general, overarching idea that allows them to sell anything they ever create to anyone who might want to buy it.

It's a search for what I call the *Magic Umbrella*.

How do they expect to cut through the Noise with an idea so big and so general it could be used to promote just about anything to anyone? Great question, yet the search continues.

This search for the Magic Umbrella often leads to meaningless corporate slogans, like:

Empowering People

Enjoy Better

Be Your Way

Look Again

Live Your Life

You Got People

Such slogans are forgettable and can't be linked to any one company because they don't even express an idea that's clear, let alone compelling.

It's easy to laugh at meaningless corporate slogans, yet, as thought leaders, we make this same mistake every day.

We look for an idea for our business that allows us to sell virtually anything we ever create to anyone who is willing to buy it.

We're looking for a Magic Umbrella that encompasses everything we could ever do, say, or sell.

To me, this search is more about us and what we want to do, instead of the people we want to lead, the people who just want to understand who we are, what we're selling, and what makes us different.

When we take our Magic Umbrella idea and put it in front of potential clients, it has the same impact as a meaningless corporate slogan.

*Magic Umbrella ideas don't cut through the Noise.*

So what kind of idea cuts through the Noise?

A Clear & Compelling Idea.

I've come to believe that the quality of our idea dictates our ceiling of success. There are some great, classic examples like FedEx, Domino's Pizza, and BMW.

"Overnight" was the idea behind the explosive growth of FedEx.

"30-minute delivery or it's free" did the same for Domino's Pizza.

The "Ultimate Driving Machine" was the idea that catapulted BMW past Mercedes in luxury car sales.

Thought leaders have the same challenge.

*What Is Our Clear & Compelling Idea?*

The goal is to have an idea at the heart of our business that is so clear and compelling to our ideal clients that they can't help themselves. They *must* learn more.

To understand what makes an idea clear and compelling, it's helpful to look at what happens when our idea is anything less than clear and compelling.

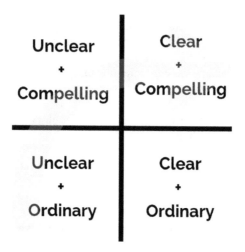

**Clear & Ordinary**—This is the most common. Imagine if we ran a local service business: accountant, insurance salesperson, financial advisor, or real estate agent. It's very clear what we sell, but we're also viewed as a commodity.

This causes price-shopping and lack of loyalty. Prospects are in control because they don't view us as irreplaceable. We end up begging for business, cutting fees, making deals, offering discounts, and compromising profits just to stay in business.

**Unclear & Ordinary**—As bad as Clear & Ordinary is, being Unclear & Ordinary is by far the worst. Not only is it unclear what we do, but when people finally understand what we do, it turns out to be ordinary. There's nothing compelling about it. No reason to take action and learn more.

We're like a restaurant that tries to please everyone, yet ends up serving a bunch of ordinary dishes no one gets excited about.

When we have an unclear, ordinary idea, the results show up in lots of ways, from slow growth and few referrals, to little enthusiasm from prospects when we explain our service. There's an overall sluggishness around the business. It feels like we're pushing a giant rock up a very steep hill. If we find ourselves in this category, we should get out of it as quickly as possible.

**Unclear & Compelling**—This is where most thought leaders live. We *are* unique. We *do* have compelling ideas. We are different from our competitors, but those differences are not razor-sharp clear to our Audience.

It's actually easier to fall into this trap when we have multiple skills, interests, and abilities.

Our wide range of skills, interests, and abilities lead us away from focusing on solving one problem. Because we have the ability to serve multiple types of people, we believe we should. We end up being a jack of all trades and master of none. Which is great if we're building our own house, not so great if we're trying to cut through the Noise.

The results of being Unclear & Compelling often look like this: We sell best from speaking gigs, live events, personal relationships, and referrals, but we have difficulty scaling beyond that.

We have compelling differences from our opponents, but it takes time for people to understand those differences. People need large chunks of time or high-trust referrals before they buy from us.

In other words, Unclear & Compelling is another category we should escape as quickly as possible.

**Clear & Compelling**—Now we are in the domain of the thought leaders who have broken through. We've boiled our insight and creativity down into an idea that is compelling and *razor-sharp clear* to our Audience. When the right people hear our Clear & Compelling Idea, they can't un-hear it. And they must take action. They must learn more.

What does a Clear & Compelling Idea look like in the world of thought leaders?

- Start with Why (Simon Sinek)

- Start working *on* your business instead of just *in* your business (E-Myth)

- Any marketing which fails to generate a response is a waste of money (Dan Kennedy)

- You're just "one funnel away" from success (Russell Brunson)

- Turn strangers into friends and friends into customers (Seth Godin)

- These ideas were so clear and compelling that once they got out, *their audience couldn't un-hear them.* People were compelled to take action.


## A Clear & Compelling Idea....

* Communicates quickly—it can often be boiled down to one to two sentences, speaking immediately and magnetically to the right people.

* Attracts attention and publicity—it doesn't need to be pushed as much through paid advertising.

* Spreads much easier—it can be carried along by word of mouth.

* Polarizes—it often causes disagreement, even anger and hatred, creating both loyal followers and fervent opponents.

* Creates demand—it puts laser focus on the problem we solve, stirring up demand for a solution.

* Compels the right people to take action—they must learn more, and in learning about our Idea, they often decide we are best-suited to deliver the solution to their problem.

Ideally, our Clear & Compelling Idea reframes the problem we solve or expresses a fresh new solution to the problem. That way, when our ideal client hears our Idea, their reaction is, *I must learn more!*

When we systematically deliver a Clear & Compelling Idea that speaks directly to the problem we solve, we start to become *known* for our Idea. The faster we become known for our Clear & Compelling Idea, the faster we become MicroFamous.

# Build Real Influence through Authority, Visibility & Relationships

It's not enough to attract attention or even build an audience.

In the world of thought leaders, the deciding factor in building a simple, profitable business is our ability to drive sales.

Unfortunately, attention doesn't translate directly to sales. If it did, every social media "influencer" would be rich. There's a missing link between attention and sales.

That missing link is influence.

Without influence, people may give their attention, but they don't give their trust and they don't take action.

On the other hand, MicroFamous is a strategy designed to build real influence, the kind of influence that rests on a foundation of Authority, Visibility, & Relationships.

To build influence, we must be perceived as an authority in our space, we must be visible consistently, and we must build a network of relationships with other influencers so our Audience understands where we fit in.

Let's look at each element of influence. Then we'll look at what happens when we're missing one of these foundational elements.

## Authority

As a society, we've been on the receiving end of media messages for well over a hundred years. Every day, we're exposed to hundreds or thousands of brand images, headlines, slogans, commercials, and ads.

Each one is making a promise, yet our experience is that few deliver on their promise. As a result, we've become skeptical, cynical, and downright jaded.

Yet, we still have problems we want solved. We're always scanning, looking for solutions to problems from people we can trust.

Our people are no different. They are always scanning, looking for solutions to problems in their business and life. They want to work with a respected leader, someone who has authority and credibility, someone to whom others look for leadership.

These types of social cues are often the only way people can tell who is a true leader and who is pretending.

As thought leaders, our tendency is to try to prove we are better. We want to prove that we've mastered our craft, that we're more skilled than our competitors, that we have more expertise.

The problem is, the people we want to serve aren't experts in our space. How could they ever really know if we're the expert we claim to be?

So, people look for indicators of authority, which help them sort out the real from the fake, the pros from the amateurs, the honest from the liars.

We must always remember that if people had our skills and experience, they wouldn't need us. They wouldn't hire us to lead them to the results they want. They're in the dark, they're frustrated, and they're in pain. So, they're looking for ways to determine who to trust.

Authority is the answer.

Authority is our credibility, demonstrated expertise, and reputation among other leaders. Authority helps bridge the gap in credibility and builds trust with the right people. Authority helps them feel comfortable taking the next step with us.

That's why Authority is the first element of influence. Let's move on to the second.

## Visibility

Visibility means taking our authority and projecting it into the world. Of the three elements of influence, it's the lowest-hanging fruit. Take any business, make it more visible to potential clients, and sales will probably go up. As a result, this is often where most thought leaders focus.

However, visibility alone doesn't build influence. We need to be visible consistently and congruently. We must be visible in ways that are authentic to us and congruent with our position of authority and leadership.

As a thought leader, landing a starring role in a popular reality show might give us massive Visibility, yet it's not consistent or congruent. It doesn't reinforce our authority; it doesn't deliver our Clear & Compelling Idea to the right people; and it doesn't address the problem we solve. So, it does little to build influence.

In the world of new media, most of our best results come from consistent, congruent visibility over time. So it's critical that we're consistently visible in the places the right people are paying attention, in a way that is congruent with our position as a thought leader.

When we show up as a thought leader and systematically deliver a Clear & Compelling Idea to the right people, we become more than visible. We become famously influential.

## Relationships

Most of us recognize that we need more Visibility, and we know we need to build Authority so the right people can trust the promises we make.

Yet only a very small group of thought leaders look at influence through the lens of Relationships. Because this perspective is so uncommon, we have a huge opportunity.

In the Battle of Attention, people are always keeping track of social status.

Who is a leader, who is a follower, who is unknown? Whether they do it consciously or not, people are always scanning, building stories, and creating pecking orders built on perceptions—both their own and the perceptions of others.

So, besides the obvious benefits of relationships—referrals, co-marketing efforts and joint ventures—there's a key psychological benefit of building relationships with other influencers. A benefit that helps us become famously influential.

When we build relationships through public conversations with influencers—like podcast hosts—we can change the perception of our social status.

When we have public conversations with influencers, people pick up a variety of small social cues and signals.

They notice how a podcast host introduces us. They notice if the host defers to us or talks over us. They notice if we are consistently featured on podcasts, or if we come and go. They notice when we are universally respected by other influencers.

All this input is picked up at the subconscious level, yet these social cues help people form a perception of social status. By changing that perception, we can claim a position of leadership.

At first, that leadership position is just a perception in the minds of the right people. However, that perception can then be converted into market share through sales, which always come easier to the perceived leader. Perception first, then convert the perception into sales.

TIPPING
POINT

STAGES of INFLUENCE

# Get Known:
# The Three Stages of Influence

We don't need to be famous everywhere to make a big impact. Who wants to be so famous that we can't go out to dinner without being hounded for autographs?

The goal is to be MicroFamous.

*In other words, famously influential to a specific group of like-minded people. The people we want to teach, train, and lead.*

That might involve signing some autographs, but at industry events, not the grocery store.

As we systematically deliver our Clear & Compelling Idea to the right people, we progress through the Three Stages of Influence:

Get seen.
Get noticed.
Get KNOWN.

Here's what these stages look like in real life.

We start by being seen. We put ourselves and our message into the world by talking about the problem we solve and by sharing what we're learning and doing along the way. We share personal experiences, stories, and anecdotes, focusing on the frustrations of our ideal clients.

As we get more clarity and focus, we start to zero in on our Clear & Compelling Idea. We hear what resonates with our Audience and other thought leaders. We see what gets them talking, what gets them paying attention, what makes them reach out. We get better at sharing our Clear & Compelling Idea with others, in person and online.

Along the way, repetition leads to recognition. We go from being seen to being noticed. People start to recognize us, linking us to our Clear & Compelling Idea. We can tell it's resonating with the Audience we want to reach, and it's gaining traction in our niche.

Because we can see it working, we lean into it. We keep hammering away at our Clear & Compelling Idea, driving it home over and over again.

We start backing up our Idea by sharing the results we're getting for clients through success stories. We start getting featured on more podcast interviews, recognized by more people, and other thought leaders start coming to us. We can feel the momentum building, like a treadmill accelerating under our feet.

As we stay consistent and persistent, our influence hits a tipping point. We go from being noticed to being KNOWN. The collective perception of us and our position in our niche changes.

As we hit the tipping point of influence, things start to happen to us that didn't happen before:

- We get invited to podcast interviews, rather than pitching ourselves
- We get recognized publicly by other thought leaders in our niche and mentioned as an emerging thought leader
- We get invited to speak at events
- We get featured in industry articles, "Best Of" posts, virtual summits, webinars, and other forms of new media
- We get pitched on collaborations, joint ventures, new projects, and new business ideas
- We hear our Clear & Compelling Idea being repeated back to us by other thought leaders and potential clients

- We get recommendations and referrals from people who don't know us well—based mostly on our Clear & Compelling Idea

**In other words, we build Authority, Visibility & Relationships, which translate into real influence.**

And our influence starts to convert into sales, clients, and results.

As we continue to build influence, we go from being seen, to being noticed, to being KNOWN.

Just as John Maxwell is known for leadership, or Kim Scott is known for radical candor, or Seth Godin is known for marketing, we become known for our Clear & Compelling Idea.

That's what it looks like to become MicroFamous: we have built real, enduring influence with a group of like-minded people we want to serve and impact.

So, if the benefit is so compelling, vivid, and clear, what keeps us from becoming MicroFamous? Why are so many thought leaders struggling to get attention, create demand, and attract more clients? I believe there are several reasons...

First, we try to be everything to everyone.

We believe that if we focus on one niche, we are forever locked in that niche and can't grow and expand. This isn't true; we can always grow and expand.

Second, we (wildly) overestimate how much people pay attention to us.

People get hit with a staggering number of media messages and brand impressions every day, so they are probably not hearing from us often enough to get sick of us.

Third, we underestimate what it takes to progress through the Three Stages of Influence.

Especially when it comes to *focus*. It takes focus to hit the tipping point from being noticed to being KNOWN.

Hitting the tipping point is like trying to fill an empty bucket with water. To hit the tipping point, we have to put so much water into the bucket that it overflows. The more buckets we try to fill, the longer it takes to fill any one of those buckets.

This is what we do when we try be everything to everyone, or try to be visible everywhere our people might be paying attention.

Everything we do on new media—every podcast episode, every interview, every social media post—that doesn't help us become famously influential to the right people is a distraction. A dilution of our efforts.

By focusing on the right people, being visible on the platforms where they are paying attention, and systematically delivering our Clear & Compelling Idea, we give ourselves the best chance of hitting that tipping point of influence.

We know we've hit that tipping point when we become KNOWN for our Clear & Compelling Idea. We become linked to it, synonymous with it. That's how real, enduring influence is built.

# SHRINK
*the*
# BATTLEFIELD

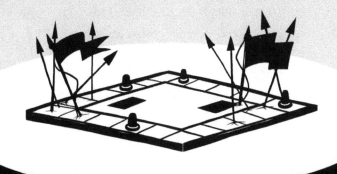

# Shrink the Battlefield

As thought leaders, we get to choose where we fight the Battle for Attention, attract an audience, and build influence.

Just as great military generals carefully choose where to fight, rigging battles by shrinking the battlefield to favor their strengths, we can rig the Battle for Attention in our favor.

We do this by choosing a niche—a specialized segment of a market.

And not just any niche.

A niche we can *own*. A niche where we can become the recognized leader.

A niche where we become the natural, obvious choice for the right people.

Shrinking the battlefield means starting with a focused, defined niche rather than the larger market we eventually want to reach. And that's okay. Just because we start in a focused niche doesn't mean we're limiting ourselves forever.

Music is a great example of this approach. Think of any band that achieves mainstream success. When we dig into their story, we always find that they built an engaged fanbase first and then "broke out" into the mainstream. Great bands shrink the battlefield by creating music for a smaller group, creating raving fans, and those fans help them break out into mainstream success.

Here are four options to shrink the battlefield and rig the Battle for Attention in our favor.

## Creation

When we create a new niche, we select a group of people that don't currently think of themselves as a niche. People who are ignored, underserved, or taken for granted.

The key is to go where the market is heading, not where it is. That requires observation of the market, insight into the changing tastes of our Audience, lots of clear thinking, and some good luck on the timing.

But when we create the right niche, we position ourselves to benefit from explosive growth.

That's what Mark Amtower did when he created a niche called "government marketing." Mark helps bring companies together with the government agencies who need their products and services. This niche ended up exploding as government size and budgets ballooned.

Years later, he's still the leading thought leader in that niche and reinforces his leadership position with radio, podcasting, guest articles, and media appearances.

Creating a new niche requires courage, yet it is often where we find the least competition and fastest growth.

## Combination

We can also shrink the battlefield by combining existing niches into a more focused and defined niche.

A classic example is Dan Kennedy, who became a leader in the "direct response marketing" niche. He didn't just set out to be a marketing expert for small businesses; he built a Clear & Compelling Idea around "direct response" and why it's the most effective form of marketing for small businesses and entrepreneurs.

Direct response wasn't new, and neither was small business marketing. But no one combined them to form a distinct niche, which left a gap in the market for Dan to claim as his own.

Blending existing elements allows us to play with powerful ideas, concepts, and niche markets that are already trending. When the right elements come together, we can create a fast-growing niche that feels like a natural outgrowth of established trends.

## Reframe & Reposition

When we position other thought leaders as dinosaurs who are out of touch, we shrink the battlefield by appealing to the young and repelling the old. This can be done regardless of real age, by creating a niche that appeals to those who want to be young.

Glenn Twiddle, one of the top real estate coaches and thought leaders in Australia, did this by combining business coaching, social media, and local events to help real estate agents become local celebrities.

By itself that has a certain level of appeal, but he didn't stop there. Taking a page from the Dan Kennedy playbook, Glenn positioned himself as the "renegade" real estate coach and repositioned his competing coaches as dinosaurs—behind the times and hopelessly out of touch.

As a result, he attracts energetic, like-minded clients who want to try new things. In other words, he used reframing and repositioning to create a niche that magnetically draws his ideal clients.

## Opposition

By picking out some attribute of our competition and doing the opposite, we carve out a niche that magnetically draws like-minded people, people who are underserved by the other thought leaders in our niche.

This is the approach Jackie Chan took when he set out to do the opposite of everything Bruce Lee did. Where Lee's fighting style made him seem invincible, Jackie would wince and show vulnerability, even to the point of comedy. In the process, he carved out a new niche that he could own—martial arts comedy.

What Jackie did is one of the toughest things in the world—becoming an international superstar in a niche already dominated by one of the greatest icons of all time. It all started by doing the opposite.

We can also see this in the sales trainers that came out against the cold calling, hardcore closing attitude of the '80s.

They positioned themselves as relationship- and referral-based and, as a result, attracted the people who were neglected or repelled by a "Glengarry Glenn Ross" approach to sales. They did the opposite and became MicroFamous.

When I talk with other thought leaders about carving out a niche they can own, I often get this response: "But I don't want to be huge."

My response is always, "Do you want to be profitable?"

It's been shown that the leading brand in any niche captures the majority of the economics of that niche, especially profit. Right behind that is the #2 brand, and everyone else fights for the scraps.

In other words, profit is a direct result of being a leader in a profitable niche. And the majority of the profit goes to the brand that comes to mind *first*.

In the world of thought leaders, the leader in a niche captures most of the profit in that niche because they tend to get the best clients, land the best speaking engagements, sell the most books, and own the most critical relationships.

So if the goal isn't to be huge, why not embrace it? Shrink the battlefield. Focus on becoming MicroFamous in a specialized segment of the market. A niche we can own, not just compete in.

*For the research on category kings and profit, see Play Bigger by Christopher Lochhead. Harper Collins 2016

# Choose Who to Serve

Even once we Shrink the Battlefield and choose the niche we want to own, our first instinct is to appeal to everyone in that niche.

It's like there's a constant internal pressure to be everything to everyone.

Family and friends tell us to "diversify" and avoid alienating anyone who could possibly buy from us.

We watch established thought leaders get drawn off course, expanding their brand and broadening their message to the point where they lose the very thing that made them unique.

We must remember that in any niche, the people break down into two groups—the Many and the Few.

**The Many are the majority, the mainstream of that niche.**

The ones doing what the majority are doing and getting the results the majority are getting.

**The Few are the minority—the rebels.**

The ones who go against the grain, doing things differently, and getting different results (and usually far better results).

The Few are the ones who tend to...

- go against the crowd and try new things
- suffer from fewer limiting beliefs
- be more resourceful

- take action when they believe it will get them better results

They are the current and emerging leaders. They love new ideas, new strategies, new products, and new services. They care more about getting results than about being right. They are often the early adopters.

Contrast that with the Many, who tend to be...

- risk-averse, preferring to be led rather than lead
- hampered by limiting beliefs
- less resourceful
- reluctant to take decisive action

The Many are the middle and late adopters, looking around for social proof, evidence, and success stories, before they take action. Not exactly the first ones to jump on a new idea.

The Few and the Many have different habits and beliefs.

They take different actions and get different results. Because of these differences, they also make buying decisions differently.

The Few is where we'll find the most driven, successful, and respected people in any niche. The Few are the first to experiment with new strategies, methods, systems, and tactics. They have the performance discipline to put in the work and expect a reward later. They can handle the pressure of going a different direction than the rest of their industry.

These are the very people who probably get the best results from our service, and they will be our biggest champions once they see the results. Because they're among the most successful and respected people in the niche, when they publicly endorse something, everyone pays attention.

As a result, the Few is often where we'll find the best potential clients in our niche.

What does this have to do with our becoming MicroFamous? Can't we just speak to both?

We could try, but it's hard to find a Clear & Compelling Idea that resonates with both the Few *and* the Many.

**What makes an idea "compelling" is subjective.**

A Clear & Compelling Idea to the Many often isn't advanced enough for the Few. And a Clear & Compelling Idea to the Few can be too polarizing or advanced for the Many.

So, if we agree that the Audience in any niche breaks down into the Many and the Few, we have a decision to make.

WHO do we serve?

Because the Many and the Few make buying decisions very differently, we must choose who to serve in order to deliver a truly Clear & Compelling Idea.

Do we go exclusive, serving the Few, and risk excluding the Many? Do we go mainstream, serving the Many, and risk turning off the Few?

This can be a hard decision to make. Which is why many of us don't decide at all. We simply lump everyone together—speaking to the Many and the Few as if they shared the same habits, beliefs, and buying processes.

Yet this decision is the key to uncovering our Clear & Compelling Idea, the one thing for which we want to become known. We must choose. Do we serve the Few or the Many?

# Specialize for Ideal Clients

As the economy creates more options and customization, the trend in every area, from consumer goods to coaching and consulting, is to specialize.

To create solutions that are custom-tailored to an audience and their version of a problem.

Specialization is a force, like a powerful current. Our challenge is to move with the current, not against it.

All other factors being equal, loan officers will choose a mortgage coach over a business coach. Real estate agents will choose a real estate trainer over a sales trainer. CEOs of manufacturing companies looking to scale will choose consultants who specialize in helping manufacturers scale.

This is all rooted in human nature.

People in every niche feel their problem is unique and different. So, we seek out unique solutions, even if the main difference is the packaging and presentation.

Cough medicine is the perfect example. The ingredients are mostly the same, yet the packaging is tailor-made for every possible variety of the problem. According to a quick check of WebMD, there are over 4,400 drugs and medications that can be used to treat a cough:

Nighttime, daytime, fast-acting, slow release, congestion, allergies, the list goes on. Virtually any combination of symptoms has its own medicine.

Specialization is a force, rewarding the specialists and often driving out the generalists.

Selling a general solution in a world that rewards specialization is like swimming upstream. It's not impossible, but definitely more difficult.

This current, this force of specialization, applies to us as thought leaders in a few key ways.

Niche groups of people tend to fragment, not converge.

Executives and business media types are constantly looking for convergence and synergy, yet they rarely work in real life.

Software is a great example. When software companies try to build all-in-one platforms, the result is usually slow, bloated software that isn't great at any one thing.

Technology is another great example. So far, the closest we've come to the "convergence" of the PC and the TV has been the latest generation of "smart" TVs that allow us to watch cat videos on YouTube in stunning high definition.

Why? Because specialized solutions are better than a catch-all solution that tries to be good at everything. This force of specialization works 24/7 against convergence and synergy.

Yet every day, companies are merged or acquired, endless variations of brands are introduced, and domestic products are launched in foreign countries, with mostly terrible results.

Every day, thought leaders follow the lead of those companies and launch new products, programs, and services, all based on the ideas of convergence and synergy, and get the same terrible results.

For thought leaders, convergence and synergy are poor bets. Our better bet is to assume that the niches we operate in will fragment into smaller niches over time, and base our business around that assumption.

Niches tend to reward (and even demand) specialized solutions.

If specialization is like a river current, then offering specialized services is like swimming with the current.

We do this by syphoning off the right people and creating a specialized solution just for them.

People are naturally drawn to solutions that are tailor-made for them, so going with the current of specialization gives us an unfair advantage over the generalists in our niche.

Niches offer endless ways to specialize, but not every specialization matters to the audience.

That's why it can difficult to "break out" from a focused niche into a larger one. Taking a specialized solution to a wider audience runs the risk of losing the very elements that made our solution unique and compelling in the first place.

When we move into a larger niche, our first instinct is to strip out some of the specialization. For example,

Mortgage coaches try to become small business coaches

Small business coaches try to become corporate consultants

Corporate consultants try to become life coaches

Life coaches try to become motivational speakers

In trying to appeal to a wider audience, we often end up running counter to the natural human desire for a specialized solution.

It's like venturing into a deeper part of a river, with a more powerful current, and then shifting to swim against the current. If we're not careful, we actually lose the advantage of being the specialist.

So, what's the answer? Are we forever locked into a defined niche, where we our specialization keeps us from breaking out?

Of course not.

We can all point to thought leaders who are leaders in niches so big it's hard to even think of them as niches. Seth Godin (marketing), Grant Cardone (sales), and John Maxwell (leadership) are all great examples.

They found a way to specialize even in large, highly competitive niches. By chance or by design, they hit upon a specialization that matters to a wide audience. As a result, they captured a leadership position in a large niche, or multiple niches.

We can do the same thing. The key is to find a type of specialization that resonates with a larger audience.

Specialization is a force. As thought leaders, our challenge is to with the current, not against it. Be the Specialist, not the Generalist.

# Build a
# HOME
# BASE

# Build a Home Base

Fighting the Battle for Attention takes resources: time, energy, and capital.

If it takes all of our time, energy, and capital to cover personal needs and overhead, it leaves little left to fight the Battle for Attention.

To fight to win, we need profit. That means we need a Home Base first.

**Home Base is a leadership position we've built with a specific group of like-minded people within our defined niche.** These people make up a slice of the niche that's small enough to be captured, but valuable enough to generate a sustainable profit.

It's like a base camp in the Battle of Attention.

The fastest way to build a Home Base is skip the Many and serve the Few—the most valuable slice of a niche—and serve them at a high level. This allows us to experiment and develop our tools and systems quickly. This is where we can dig in and deliver big results to early adopter clients.

As we get results for the Few, they spread the word and introduce us to other people. Soon we have a core group of ideal clients all getting good results from our work.

As our tools and systems get better and it takes less time and effort to deliver results to that core group of clients, we start to build up profits—in time, energy, and capital. As it takes less time and effort to deliver results, the results we deliver become more valuable. So, we can raise our fees, deliver a better service, work fewer hours, and generate higher profits.

Our Home Base is also a safe harbor, giving us security and stability so we can take chances in other areas.

Starting with a Home Base is better in the long run than appealing to an entire niche right away. Our Home Base puts us in a sustainable, profitable position while laying the foundation for our next moves.

The sooner we build our Home Base, the sooner we have the full range of options for fighting to win, and the profits from our Home Base to fund our next moves. Once we've built our Home Base, a range of options opens to us.

## Option 1: Make a Big Move

When we have put in the time, effort, and energy to build a Home Base, our Home Base starts to give *back* to us. We are serving the most valuable slice of the market, so we get profits back in more than just cash; we also gain profits of time and energy.

If we don't spend our profits, they start to stockpile. We have more time, energy, and capital on our hands.

This creates the option to take that stockpile and use it to launch a Big Move—a campaign to capture a leadership position in a larger niche.

## Option 2: Widen the Moat

In other words, we can continue to eliminate competition, raise our fees, and increase our average client quality.

Peter Drucker is a perfect example of widening the moat. Once he became known for "management," he reinforced his leadership position by continually writing and speaking around management concepts. He developed new, powerful ideas that built a bigger moat around his leadership position.

As a result, he became an icon.

His ideas became so revered around the world that no one could break the link between Drucker and "management."

This wasn't pre-ordained by the gods, and it didn't happen by accident. Drucker did it by hammering away at the same niche for decades.

If we're fortunate to choose a niche that continues to grow and mature throughout our lifetime, we may be able to follow in Drucker's footsteps and invest our profits into widening the moat around our Home Base.

## Option 3: Be the Champion of Our Niche

In contrast to widening the moat, being the Champion of our niche means systematically delivering our Clear & Compelling Idea to a larger audience outside our Home Base. *We grow our niche by bringing new people in.*

Gary Keller, founder and CEO of Keller Williams, worked this strategy to perfection on multiple levels. When Gary and co-author Jay Papasan published *The Millionaire Real Estate Agent*, they created a new vision of success in real estate.

This put real estate sales in front of people outside the industry, pulling them in and growing the entire niche of real estate salespeople.

A niche is a living entity that is born, grows and matures. We can help fuel that growth process by becoming the Champion of our niche. Because we have a Home Base in that niche, serving the most successful and respected clients, we become famously influential to more people as the niche grows.

## Option 4: Retreat When Necessary

If any of our future moves are unsuccessful, we can fall back to our Home Base. This is especially true when our Home Base accounts for most (or all) of our personal income. This level of personal security and stability allows us to make good decisions, since we're free from fear and anxiety over our personal income.

When we focus on building our Home Base first, we are not limiting ourselves. We're actually opening up additional options. The profits of our Home Base create the stockpile of resources that allow us to choose one of these options to serve and impact more people.

So, if our goal is to build a simple, profitable business, start by building a Home Base.

# Turn Attention into Demand

For many thought leaders, there is a key point where we stall out.

We're sharing good content, and we're getting lots of encouragement, but we aren't getting sales.

Unfortunately, this is more common than we'd like to admit, especially in the world of podcasting.

There are many "influencers" who can attract attention but can't create sales.

How is this possible?

How can we attract attention without creating sales?

For the answer, let's look at two contrasting examples of influence.

We'll start with the iconic Barbara Walters. While being one of the world's most famous and skilled interviewers, would you think of her for business coaching? Probably not.

All the attention she gained in her niche worked perfectly to build her personal brand, but that attention mainly created demand for more interviews.

On the other end of the spectrum we have Jason Klein, co-founder of Brandiose. Jason and his co-founder started the first design/branding agency to specialize in minor league sports teams.

They had a Clear & Compelling Idea: minor league teams should reflect the significance of their hometowns. This idea is both positive and polarizing because the traditional approach was to focus on the link to their parent teams, which were often hundreds or thousands of miles away.

The average sports fan has never heard of Brandiose, which is exactly the point. The Brandiose team stepped into a defined niche, claimed a leadership position, and then become MicroFamous in their niche.

They created content that did more than just attract attention. They continually drove home their Clear & Compelling Idea, building influence around an idea that actually creates demand for their service.

The difference between those two examples is demand.

When like-minded people hear a Clear & Compelling Idea that promises a solution to their problem, they simply can't help themselves.

They must learn more.

If we aren't seeing that response, we know our Clear & Compelling Idea needs to be sharpened.

Our Idea must be so clear, so razor-sharp to our ideal clients that it creates demand— it compels them to learn more. Anything less than Clear & Compelling might attract attention and get encouragement, yet it doesn't create demand.

It's critical not to fall into the trap of seeking attention for its own sake. For those of us who sell our expertise, the only attention that matters is the attention that builds real influence and creates real demand.

So how do we sharpen our Clear & Compelling Idea to create demand?

First, we look at what we're promising our audience.

- Are we promising a transformation?
- Are we promising to cure an injustice?
- Are we promising a new way to solve an existing problem?
- Are we promising to solve a problem everyone thinks is unsolvable?

Ideally, our Clear & Compelling Idea promises to solve a problem in a new and surprising way.

Remember the original idea of Netflix? DVDs through the mail with no late fees. They tapped into the sense of injustice people felt, while offering a new way to solve a common problem. All in just a few words.

Books that stand the test of time, like Think & Grow Rich (Napoleon Hill), Permission Marketing (Seth Godin), and Crossing the Chasm (Geoffrey Moore), all share one thing in common.

At the heart of each book is a Clear & Compelling Idea promising a new solution to a real problem. So we start by looking at what we're promising.

Second, we look for ways to be positively polarizing.

We don't need to be the James Dean of our industry to deliver a Clear & Compelling Idea. It's not about being the "rebel" type. We just need to take a stand and speak up for what we believe in. We need to "choose the hill we're willing to die on."

Do we believe something strongly that our competition would disagree with, and are we willing to take that stand in public? If not, there's work to be done on our Clear & Compelling Idea.

There is always a way to share our Idea in a way that polarizes the audience into people who agree and disagree—without being negative or inauthentic.

Third, we look at sacred cows.

These are the good ideas that are actually the enemy of our Clear & Compelling Idea. The good people we want to serve in other niches that keep us from focusing on the right people.

Are we willing to sacrifice our good ideas so we can become known for our Clear & Compelling Idea?

Are we willing to focus on becoming famously influential to the right people, and turn away everyone else?

If not, we'll find it difficult to uncover a Clear & Compelling Idea.

Finally, we look at our delivery.

What if we have the right Idea, but we don't have the right phrasing, the right expression, or the right packaging?

Our Idea won't be razor-sharp Clear and Compelling.

The good news is that the more we get featured on podcast interviews, sharing our Clear & Compelling Idea, the more we can play with our delivery. We can experiment with new phrases and expressions, finding what resonates with our Audience.

Uncovering and delivering our Clear & Compelling Idea is a process. We shouldn't worry if it doesn't come overnight. The key is to be aware of this process, so we are constantly refining, constantly moving toward our Clear & Compelling Idea.

When we have our Clear & Compelling Idea, and we systematically deliver that Idea to the right people, we turn influence into demand.

# Raise the Standard for Clients

What makes someone an ideal client?

For many companies, the standard is simple and clear. An ideal client is someone who is willing and enthusiastic to buy.

As thought leaders, we often take this same approach when selling our services. We gladly take a check from anyone who is willing and enthusiastic to work with us. Then we roll up our sleeves and get to work, attempting to generate the results we promised.

Since most of us can't do everything for our clients, we need them to take action to get results. On top of that, we probably need them to take consistent action over time to get the best results.

Unfortunately, no matter how willing and enthusiastic clients are when they first sign up, enthusiasm fades at some point.

When that happens, clients get distracted, maybe even discouraged. They start dragging their feet, bringing up other strategies, questioning our methods, looking at ways around the work required to get the best results.

Then it hits us—*they weren't the right people.*

Because they're not taking the necessary action, we can't get them the best results. When we don't get clients the best results, we don't make the impact in the world we want to make.

For most of us, an Ideal Client is more than someone willing and enthusiastic to buy. We need our clients to take consistent action over time to get the best results.

We must do more than simply sign up anyone who is willing to pay.

We should set a new standard: **An Ideal Client is a client we love** *—long after we get paid.*

And we know it's possible because it's happened to all of us at some point. A prospect shows up on our doorstep, and they're already moving in the right direction.

They already...

- believe in our Clear & Compelling Idea
- believe we have the best solution to their problem
- believe our solution is worth far more than the asking price
- believe that NOW is the time to act

The sales process moves smoothly, and we sign them up with less effort and persuasion. After we take payment, the client relationship moves faster, smoother, and easier as well.

Because they already believe in our solution, they take action and get the results we promise. We get fulfillment and satisfaction from the impact we've made, and the clients are excited and energized by their results. It's a true win-win.

That's what it's like when we work with an Ideal Client.

So, what separates an Ideal Client from others who are just enthusiastic and willing to buy?

Beliefs.

That's a strong statement, and everyone may not agree, so let's look at the evidence, starting with a few real-world examples.

Let's say we offer business coaching. We believe we can help our clients double their business in 18 months. That's our promise and we've proven by experience we can deliver those results.

What if our client believes if they actually doubled their business, their workload would also double? They would never see their family, never hit the gym, and never have free time again. They have an internal belief that doubling their business will double their work.

How does this belief affect the client relationship?

It starts when they don't raise their performance to hit their goals. They waffle on the changes they need to make, they fudge their numbers, and they hide from analyzing their failures.

In other words, they resist the very changes that would actually double their business. All because they believe something different.

Let's look at a higher-level example. Let's say we offer consulting to CEOs of high-growth companies.

We believe that in order to scale, the right people must be in the right roles. Chances are, in any company looking to scale, personnel needs some shaking up. It's one of our core beliefs for clients to get the results we promise.

What if our client believes their personnel is just fine, and, in fact, any personnel changes are off the table?

We can imagine how this internal belief plays out.

By digging in their heels, the client limits our ability to position them to scale. They don't take the necessary actions, so they don't get the results they want, and the client probably chalks this up to hiring the wrong consultant.

These situations happen all the time, and it's all due to beliefs.

We can take the same expertise, the same insight, and the same systems and strategies, and get wildly different results, all based on our clients' beliefs.

Yet there's good news. We are not powerless. We can raise the standard for clients, and attract clients we love by the content we put into the world.

# Attract Ideal Clients
# Today & Tomorrow

In any niche, whatever we sell, there are a group of people who are primed and ready to be our ideal clients.

They share similar beliefs and points of view, and they're looking for ways to solve a real problem. They're searching for videos on YouTube, looking for books and webinars on the subject, and listening to podcasts, all in an effort to find that one piece of information they need to solve their problem.

Creating new media content, like podcast interviews or hosting our own podcast, makes it easy for these ideal clients to find us. They're already looking for the information and expertise we can deliver.

While most of the people in our niche aren't Ideal Clients today, there is a huge group of people in our niche with the potential to become Ideal Clients down the road.

So, how do we attract them?

Become famously influential to the right people.

Talk about their problems, their frustrations, their pain. Share a new perspective, a new opportunity, a new solution. Be in the places they spend time, the places where they are looking for answers.

When like-minded people come across us, they are drawn to us. They want to hear from us. They give us permission to stay in touch because our content has real value.

More importantly, they want to be led to the results we promise.

By consuming our content over time, they are exposed to content that cultivates new beliefs, transforming them into Ideal Clients.

If our niche is full of like-minded people who could be Ideal Clients, why not focus on every platform where they spend time?

First, our time, energy, and focus are not infinite. We must choose where to invest.

Second, all platforms are not equal when it comes to thought leaders.

Many social platforms just aren't the right place to teach, train, and lead.

People aren't there looking for solutions.

Just like cocktail parties aren't the right place to chat with an insurance agent about policies, certain platforms don't work for engaging potential clients. And this has a huge impact. It's more difficult to monetize followers on those platforms. Not impossible, just more difficult.

Right now, if I had a choice of 100k followers on Instagram or a podcast audience of 10k, I'll take the podcast audience hands down. Why? Because people use podcasts to look for solutions to problems.

So, for thought leaders, it's best to focus on the places where the right people are looking for solutions to problems and pair that with a social media platform where we can talk to them directly.

By pairing podcasts with a social platform, we have a powerful 1-2 punch. A platform for leadership and a platform for engagement.

That's how we make it easy for Ideal Clients to find us today, while getting permission to stay in touch with like-minded people who could be Ideal Clients tomorrow.

# Craft a Point of View

As a thought leader, we are heading in a specific direction.

We know where we're going and where we want to lead our Audience. We also know that our ideal clients are those who are already moving in the same direction.

We are heading in that direction because we believe certain things.

We have a whole set of internal beliefs—about the world, about life, our industry, our niche, and our business. Beliefs about what gets results and what doesn't, what's important and what isn't.

Those beliefs form our Point of View.

Our Point of View is the way we look at the world. It's our perspective. It determines which direction we're heading, what we talk about, and what types of people we attract into our world.

When we aren't clear on our beliefs, and we haven't crafted our Point of View, we can't deliver a Clear & Compelling Idea.

We end up creating content that attracts an audience, but doesn't create new beliefs or compel people to take *action*.

There is a straight line from our Point of View to the results we experience every day in our business.

Yet we spend most of our time creating content to attract attention, without much thought to the Point of View we're sharing in our content.

If we want to become famously influential to the right people, we need a different approach.

We need to craft our Point of View.

Our Point of View sets our direction, including where we're leading people, the problem we solve, and the results we promise.

Our Point of View attracts the right people, while repelling everyone else. Over time, we build an Audience of people who share our beliefs.

Our Point of View separates us from our Opponents, eliminating competition and making us the obvious choice for people who share our beliefs.

Think of a Point of View like a pyramid.

At the top is our Clear & Compelling Idea. It's our tip of the spear into the world, the one thing for which we want to become known.

Under that is the framework of beliefs, values, and opinions about what's true and important in the world, including the beliefs people need in order to buy from us.

Each of those beliefs is supported by evidence: stories, anecdotes, statistics, and facts.

As we refine and sharpen our beliefs and uncover more convincing evidence to support those beliefs, we can craft a more powerful and effective our Point of View.

Here's what it looks like to crafting a Point of View.


**Identify all supporting beliefs.**

Beliefs rest on evidence, so we want to dig up all the supporting evidence we have. Of course, our Audience already has their own beliefs, which rest on their own evidence. What new evidence could we share that would shake their conviction and help convert them to our beliefs?

**Make each belief fight for its place.**

Pit each of our beliefs against each other and rank them. Which beliefs are the most important? Which beliefs are universal, and which are specific to us? Which beliefs do people absolutely have to share in order to become a client? (hint: these are the Buying Beliefs).

The more supporting beliefs our Audience shares, the more likely they will share the Buying Beliefs. The more Buying Beliefs they share, the fewer objections and less resistance we'll experience in the sales process.

**Seek out controversy.**

In sifting through this jumbled-up list of beliefs, look for controversy. What beliefs and opinions do you shy away from saying publicly? Where do you run counter to conventional wisdom?

The people who agree with our controversial beliefs are the easiest to cultivate into ideal clients. We become the *only* option, because we are the ones who led them to new beliefs and got them moving in a new direction.

Controversial doesn't need to be negative either. Every point of disagreement, every controversial belief or bold opinion, has a positive side. Find it and emphasize it. It's not about being negative, it's about attracting the right people and repelling everyone else.

**Identify the gaps in content.**

The beliefs we haven't shared, the evidence we need to gather, the opinions we've only whispered behind closed doors. Unless we're already bringing a steady stream of Ideal Clients into our business, there are probably gaps in our Point of View that we need to find and fill in.

**Map out the Point of View.**

Put our Clear & Compelling Idea at the top, Buying Beliefs in the middle layer, and all our supporting beliefs in the foundation layer. We have just mapped the Point of View that drives all our conversations and content.

On our podcast interviews, we emphasize the beliefs that attract like-minded people. The beliefs that grab attention and court controversy. The beliefs that separate us from our competition. The beliefs that grab our Ideal Clients and get their permission to stay in touch. We can share the stories, facts, evidence, and anecdotes that reinforce our beliefs.

When we host a podcast, we can use every episode to convey some aspect of our Point of View: a key belief that moves the right people closer to us *the* beliefs that will draw them into a deeper level of relationship and create demand for our service.

We must do more than attract attention.

We need to deliver our Point of View, create new beliefs and inspire the right people to take new action. The new action that leads to new results.

If our goal is to become MicroFamous while working with clients we love, all of our new media content must convey a Clear & Compelling Idea supported by a well-crafted Point of View.

# Build in Freedom of Movement

As our influence grows and evolves, our business tends to move in one of two directions: Narrow or Expand.

Narrow—We continue to get clarity about our business, our Ideal Client, and our goals. In the process of attracting an audience and building influence, we realize we need to Shrink the Battlefield even further and refine who the "right people" are for us.

Expand—We successfully become MicroFamous in our first niche, and we set our sights on a larger niche. We want to expand and deliver a Clear & Compelling Idea designed for a larger audience. It's time to make our Big Move.

Looking at these options in advance, we may think we're destined for one direction, but we're never really sure till we see how the market responds and how our goals change as we grow as a thought leader.

We may feel that we have the right Clear & Compelling Idea, backed by a great service that solves a real problem and delivers real return on investment (ROI) to clients. We feel like we have the right approach to attract like-minded people and create new Ideal Clients. However, we don't really know till we get feedback from real people in our niche.

We also underestimate how much our own goals can change over time. Our goals may get bigger and we want to become a leader in a bigger niche. Or we may find that we want to slow down, enjoy life more, travel, or spend time with our family. We don't know how life and business growth will affect our goals five years, or even one year, from now.

We need freedom in our strategy. We must stay flexible and capable of shifting to either Narrow or Expand our business.

In other words, we need Freedom of Movement.

Fortunately, we can build in Freedom of Movement from the beginning.

We can set a flexible MicroFamous strategy—meaning key decisions can be made along the way. As we get more feedback and experience, we can Narrow or Expand.

We can get featured in new places and platforms. We can "dial in" our visibility—where and how often we get featured. As we shift our direction, we can shift how we are being pitched to Narrow or Expand our focus.

For example, if we are currently getting featured in super-niche industry podcasts, and it's time to expand into a larger niche, we simply level up. Start pitching bigger podcasts in bigger niches.

We can also craft our business brand so that small adjustments allow us to Narrow or Expand our focus.

No matter the stage of the business, we should always be MicroFamous—famously influential to the right people. Yet we don't need 100% clarity on what our target niche and Ideal Clients look like right away. Sometimes we need time to throw some mud against the wall and see what sticks.

We don't have to make every decision up front.

# Choose Tomorrow over Today

Once we understand the power of the MicroFamous strategy, our first instinct will be to bite off more than we can chew. We know the rewards are big and valuable, and we want those rewards now.

So we set big goals.

We want to do everything at the same time. Podcasting, guest interviews, social media.

In our mind, we have this compelling vision of a magical flurry of activity, where we build a bunch of new systems, get flooded with new prospects, and transform our business in a short period of time.

So, we set a deadline and get to work.

We spin our wheels switching between tasks and projects, trying to build momentum. We realize too late that our time, energy, and resources are spread too thin.

When we reach our deadline, reality throws a bucket of ice water on us. All we have are a bunch of half-built systems.

If we're not careful, we can go through this cycle over and over again. Why is that?

I believe it's due to one very popular myth: If we generate a big enough flurry of activity in a small enough timeframe, we can produce big results without the methodical, boring consistency of attracting an audience and building influence over time.

To me, this violates a basic principle of success.

Success requires a foundation of methodical, consistent action, aided by occasional flurries of activity to hit specific deadlines along the way.

This especially applies to success as a thought leader, where we build trust with a group of people who look to us for leadership. They need our help to solve a real problem in their business. Trust isn't built overnight.

Yet each influencer, with our individual strengths and weaknesses, tends to be drawn toward one of two approaches.

Some of us produce content methodically, building trust with an audience over time. Yet when it comes time to capitalize on our momentum with a flurry of activity and action, we pull back.

Some of us are all flurry and no consistency, which does nothing to build trust with an audience over time. We try to make up for this lack of consistency with more flurries of action, which only continues to short-circuit our own influence because there's no solid foundation to stand on.

The trust of an audience is not an asset built on occasional flurries of activity. It's a long-term result in a long-term game.

The more we Choose Tomorrow over Today, the more we focus on systems.

Systems make tomorrow easier.

Each system builds on our other systems, reinforcing each other and making our efforts more consistent and effective. Systems lead to consistent action and consistent action creates momentum.

This isn't easy, especially for thought leaders. We tend to be confident, driven, and ambitious, yet we're also impatient, restless, overworked, and easily distracted by new tools and tactics.

But this is great news for those who commit to building one system at a time.

While our competition goes from day to day, scattered and distracted, we out-maneuver them with systems and consistent action over time.

Becoming MicroFamous starts with a simple commitment: Choose Tomorrow over Today.

# PART TWO
# SYSTEM

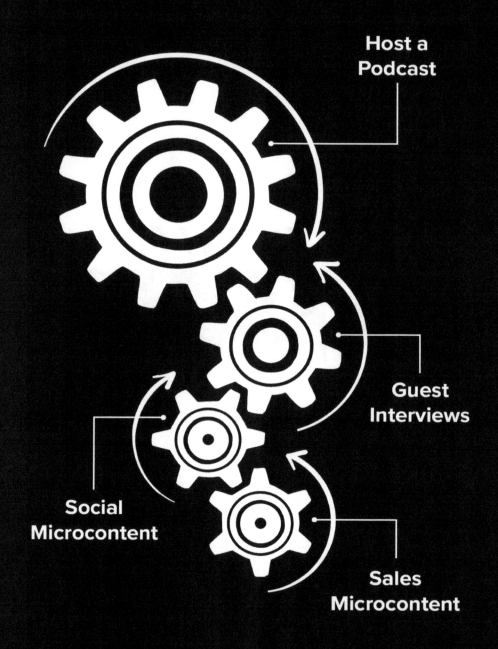

Host a
Podcast

Guest
Interviews

Social
Microcontent

Sales
Microcontent

New
**MEDIA MACHINE**

# New Media Machine

If we wake up every day asking ourselves what to post on social media, we're having the wrong conversation.

When we have a different strategy and a different system for delivering content, our conversation changes.

Instead we wake up with different questions:

- What podcast interviews are booked this month?
- How are we leveraging our podcast episodes?
- What small chunks of content are we pulling out to share on social media?
- How are we creating conversations around that content?

MicroFamous is the strategy. It sets the destination we want to reach—where we become famously influential to the right people.

The system is the vehicle that gets us to that destination. We call that system a New Media Machine.

And the New Media Machine is the ultimate vehicle for thought leaders.

New Media Machine leverages the four most effective types of new media to systematically deliver our Clear & Compelling Idea to the right people, attract an Audience, and build influence.

Let's look at the four types of new media.

**Podcast Interviews**

We start by appearing as a guest expert on podcasts, video series, webinars, or live shows. It's the easiest way to build Authority, Visibility & Relationships, the key elements of real influence.

When we get featured, we have one goal—deliver a Clear & Compelling Idea that grabs the attention of the right people and gets their permission to stay in touch.

When we deliver a Clear & Compelling Idea to an ideal client, it should generate this response; "WOW...I HAVE to learn more!"

Then we make it easy to learn more by giving permission to stay in touch, which builds a list of like-minded people who want to hear from us consistently. A permission-based email list is still one of the most powerful—and neglected—assets in a thought leader business.

## Podcast Hosting

Then we launch a podcast where we keep in touch with our email list. It's where we share our best stuff—the hyper-specific, actionable content our ideal clients are searching for right now.

Our podcast allows us to expand on our Clear & Compelling Idea, sharing a positive and polarizing Point of View with the supporting beliefs, values, and opinions that make us unique and attractive. It's where we attract those who are already ideal clients while delivering content that cultivates new ideal clients.

Yet our Podcast can't do everything. In a world of social media and short attention spans, we need two forms of micro-content.

## Micro-Content for Sales Support

This is very specific, short-form content specifically for people who raise their hand and get into our sales process.

In small chunks of audio and video, we share success stories, testimonials, excerpts from key podcasts, and live speaking engagements.

The goal is to set a vision of success, build trust, destroy objections, and overcome limiting beliefs that keep people from moving forward.

## Micro-Content for Social Media

This is short-form content designed for our social platform, where we want to create Connection, Conversation and Community. We all know that small chunks of content work better on social media—but creating all that content from scratch is a full-time job.

By putting podcasting first, our New Media Machine leverages the most fun and fulfilling form of content creation—conversations—and turns them into multiple forms of micro-content.

That allows us to spend less effort and energy creating content from scratch, and more time in conversations with our Audience. We can use social media to lead them to our podcast, where we can strengthen the relationship and cultivate ideal clients.

So, what does a New Media Machine look like when it's fully installed?

We consistently get featured on podcasts—reaching new audiences, delivering our Clear & Compelling Idea, getting their permission to stay in touch...

We host our own podcast—delivering content that builds trust, converting beliefs, and drawing them closer to where they to raise their hand...

We pull out micro-content for sales support—destroying objections, turning prospects into ideal clients, and closing more sales...

We publish micro-content for social media—creating connection, conversation and community, expanding our Audience and leading them to our podcast...

...and we combine all those into one system that works 24/7 to build Authority, Visibility & Relationships.

Now let's take a closer look at each stage of a New Media Machine.

# Get Featured on Podcast Interviews

There are thousands of ways to reach people online.

There are very few that introduce us as the trusted expert—THE authority in our field. There are even fewer that allow us to spend more than a couple minutes with the audience.

Podcast interviews give us the best of both—an introduction as the trusted expert, and 30 to 60 minutes of time to share our message with an audience.

That's why the first stage in building our New Media Machine is podcast interviews, where we leverage outside audiences, bring new people into our email list, build influence, and create demand for our service.

Let's look at the strategic benefits of podcast interviews.

**Leverage Outside Audiences**

Podcast interviews are the lowest-hanging fruit of new media. We don't need an ad budget, funnels, or pay-per-click skills. The main investment is our time. Most importantly, podcast interviews put us in front of new people—consistently and systematically.

When we speak to the same people all the time, we create pressure to come up with new things to say. To build real influence, we need to consistently deliver the same message to new people. Same message, new people.

Leveraging outside Audiences is critical at every stage of a thought leader business. No matter how big our Audience grows, we always need new, enthusiastic, like-minded people coming in. These are the people most likely to open all our emails, consume all our content, and rave about us to their friends.

## Borrow Time and Trust (ethically)

Getting featured on podcasts is a digital version of a warm introduction to a new audience. We come in as an expert—a trusted recommendation—from the host.

Trust equals promises kept over time. If we sell a high-trust service, like coaching or consulting, we can build that trust faster by getting introduced to prospects through an influencer they already trust.

When we do that, we're essentially borrowing another influencer's time they invested to build trust with their audience.

## Build Influence and Generate Demand

By giving us a platform to share our beliefs, values, and opinions, we can reach new people who agree with us.

Even if we feel like we can't handle more demand (because our business is in transition or our individual client roster is full), podcast interviews are still critical. Better to have a waiting list than an empty pipeline.

All we need is permission to keep in touch with people later. Even if we feel like our business isn't perfect, there's no reason to stay on the sidelines. We should still be getting featured, building authority and visibility, while we work out those other details behind the scenes.

## Build Confidence

For thought leaders who are hesitant or don't consider themselves "ready" to get featured on podcast interviews, here are a couple points to consider.

Clarity is in the doing. In other words, doing podcast interviews often solves the very problem of not feeling ready for podcast interviews.

Keep it simple. No matter how uncomfortable or unqualified we may feel, we can always share three things on a podcast interview: What we know, what we're doing, and what we're learning. Sharing those simple things on podcast interviews is enough to start building confidence.

The more we get featured, the more conversations we have, the confidence we build. As a result, podcast interviews get easier over time.


## Build Relationships with Fellow Influencers

Having conversations with fellow influencers, even in the earliest stages of our business, can have powerful and unexpected benefits. The people we meet on podcast interviews can become referral partners, friends, and even mentors.

Speaking from experience, the relationships I formed in the earliest stages of my business have become some of the strongest and longest-lasting relationships in my business life. When influencers help us in the early stages, there's a sense of ownership and participation in our success that can build a bond that lasts for years or decades.

As our business grows, we'll often find that the right relationships can unlock new avenues for growth. Gaining access to the right niche audiences through mastermind groups or speaking gigs often starts with knowing the right person. We might be one podcast interview away from that key relationship.

After years of working with thought leaders, I have yet to see a situation where a consistent stream of podcast interviews isn't massively beneficial.

Leveraging outside audiences, and building confidence, influence, and relationships while creating demand helps any thought leader at any stage of the game.

When we're tempted to sit on the sidelines till everything is perfect, remember that we're giving our competition a big opportunity. Our ideal clients are out there looking for a solution to their problem, and they're probably looking to podcasts for answers.

Are we going to let our competition take all the good podcast interviews, generate demand for their service, build key relationships, and attract our ideal clients just because we don't feel ready?

There's no reason to sit on the sidelines and let them have all the fun. Podcast interviews must be a consistent, systematic part of our New Media Machine.

# LAUNCH

# Launch Our Podcast

No matter how consistently we get featured, we still need our own platform.

A place where we publicly claim our position as the recognized leader in our niche. A place where we control the content, format, frequency, and calls to action.

The next stage of our New Media Machine is launching our own podcast—our online home for branded, long-form new media. As thought leaders, it's where we show up and deliver our best content.

Our podcast can be a blend of audio, video, live, and pre-recorded content. Right now, the ideal podcast is audio on iTunes and Spotify, video on YouTube, with both embedded on our website.

We can feature conversations with influencers, success stories with clients, and solo episodes where we speak directly to our Audience. We recommend recording everything in video on Zoom, which can be easily leveraged into other forms of content. The key is to find the podcast format that works best for us first.

Then we distribute our podcast on new media platforms, so our Audience can consume the podcast in a way that works best for them.

Beyond the tactical side, our podcast serves a critical function in our New Media Machine; it's a magnet that attracts like-minded people and converts them into Ideal Clients over time.

Like-minded people are drawn into our Audience in several ways.

Some find our podcast through search or word of mouth. Some find us through podcast interviews or social media. Some are referred to us and then use our podcast to check our credibility and learn about our Point of View.

In the world of MicroFamous, we are only concerned with like-minded people. The goal of our podcast is not to attract the largest possible audience.

Some people simply aren't like-minded. They will never agree with our Clear & Compelling Idea, they will never share our beliefs, and they come for the wrong reasons.

In other words, they will never become ideal clients. Let them come and go. Our podcast isn't for them.

The function of a podcast is to build an Audience of like-minded people. Some will be ideal clients now; the rest will need cultivating.

Once we have an Audience of like-minded people, our podcast draws them closer to a client relationship by:

- Building authority and trust
- Setting a vision of the results we promise
- Communicating in a relentless rhythm
- Delivering content that cultivates new beliefs
- Offering clear calls to action

We'll look more at the tactics of podcasting later, for now let's look at how we can give our new podcast the best chance to attract an Audience of like-minded people.


**Build the podcast our ideal clients are looking for.**

Step outside our goals, our interests, our motivations, and put others first. Talk to our ideal clients and find out where they hang out online, their favorite forms of new media, their favorite places for business development content, and the types of content they consume daily.

For small, lucrative niches, in-depth content is the key. To reach current ideal clients, we must deliver the content they are looking for, but can't find. What content are they not getting from other podcasts, or what are they sifting through a bunch of other content to uncover?

Look for ways to give them exactly what they are looking for; the content they would happily pay for. That's the best way to create a podcast that grows fast because it answers a real, urgent need in the market.

**Build our podcast for the niche we want to own.**

Don't try to appeal to everyone. The smaller and more focused our podcast, the better chance it has to cut through the Noise and reach the right people.

By creating our podcast to appeal only to the right people, we can tailor every aspect of our podcast, including branding, content and promotion. Once we become MicroFamous to those people, other options open up, and we can shift our podcast in new directions if we choose.

**Build our podcast around our Clear & Compelling Idea.**

The foundation of all growth is word of mouth. If our Audience can't repeat the Clear & Compelling Idea of our podcast to others, either we don't have the right idea or we haven't hammered it home often enough.

We know we're getting somewhere when our Audience repeats our Clear & Compelling Idea back to us and shares the show online using our exact language and phrasing.

**Build around relentless rhythm.**

More content isn't better. Better content and more promotion is better.

To build trust, we need to communicate with our Audience in a relentless, consistent rhythm. We need to show up every week, for months and years. That's a big commitment, so we should only commit to what is sustainable for us.

Podcasts take time to find an Audience, so the biggest results of our podcast typically start around the 12- to 18-month mark.

The focus of the first 6 to 12 months of our podcast should be on improving the quality of our content and building good relationships with guests, supported by consistent guest interviews on other podcasts. This ensures that we consistently leverage outside audiences and pull them into our podcast.

Remember that the function of our podcast in the New Media Machine is to build an Audience of like-minded people. Some will be ideal clients now, the rest will need cultivating. Our podcast is the incubator, the result is ideal clients.

# Weekly Podcast Formula

If you ask 10 podcast hosts about their formula, you'll get 10 opinions on what's best for podcasting:

All interviews, zero interviews, long episodes, 5-minute episodes, Alexa Flash Briefings, self-podcasting from an iPhone. You name it, people have tried it, and everyone has an opinion.

There's nothing wrong with any of those approaches, but they aren't all equal when it comes to building influence, converting beliefs over time, and creating demand for a thought leader business.

To do that, I believe there's a formula that is not only effective but also sustainable for most thought leaders over the long run.

In our Weekly Podcast Formula, we choose from the following types of episodes so we release a new episode every week.

- Influencer Conversations

- Success Stories

- Solo Episodes

Let's look at each type of episode and its function.

## Influencer Conversations

This type of episode is built on 30- to 40-minute conversations with fellow influencers. These are people at or above our level, respected experts in their own right, who bring valuable content and can potentially share the conversation with their Audience.

Ideally, these influencers share some of our key beliefs, so when they show up and deliver their message, they align with the beliefs we're trying to cultivate in our Audience.

The purpose of these episodes is to have a real, authentic conversation with a fellow expert on a topic that can help lead our people to the results we promise and help the Audience see where this topic fits into the bigger picture of our Point of View.

And that is part of why we don't call them "interviews."

Remember, we are not Barbara Walters. The purpose of these episodes isn't to get people to cry or reveal something they hadn't planned to reveal. Leave that to the professional interviewers. Not just because it's a skillset built over a lifetime, but more importantly, doing so positions us as an interviewer instead of a thought leader.

If we are driven to teach, train and lead, our role in a conversation is not to be the best interviewer. Our role is to have a real, authentic conversation with a fellow influencer on a topic that reinforces our Point of View and helps lead our people to the results we promise.

Influencer Conversations allow us to:

- Reach out to people we may never meet otherwise
- Spend quality time learning about their business and building rapport
- Demonstrate our expertise and experience by asking insightful questions
- Add value by putting them in front of our Audience
- Generate goodwill and allow the Law of Reciprocity to kick in

- Give them a great experience with us and our team by the way we handle the podcast booking and recording process

Better yet is the effect these conversations have on the Audience.

When we have conversations with influencers, both at our level and above, here's what happens....

*Authority*—By having a peer-to-peer conversation, influencers are allowing us to borrow a portion of their credibility and authority, especially when they obviously treat us and interact with us as a colleague rather than an interviewer.

Remember, our Audience is always scanning, trying to determine the pecking order of thought leaders in a niche. They're looking for someone to solve their problem, and they want to know who is respected by other influencers and who is the recognized leader in a niche that matters to them.

*Relationship*—Podcast conversations often create a deeper and more meaningful bond than if we had met in person at an event. This sets us up for a real, meaningful relationship that can be accelerated when we do see them in person.

In fact, meeting influencers on our podcast first creates more opportunities to meet in person at the next event rather than trying to initiate new relationships at events.

Relationships are critical because those influencers are the ones who can send us a consistent stream of referrals for the next five, ten, fifteen years. They can promote our products or services to their people, put us on their stages, feature us on their podcast, and so much more.

*Leadership*—Podcast conversations naturally give and take, where our message doesn't get lost in the guest's point of view. In a real conversation, we can disagree, give a different perspective, or even play devil's advocate. We don't have to constantly shine a spotlight on the guest; we can still convey our Point of View in the conversation.

That's critical because our Audience doesn't need a thousand ideas; they need leadership, and we can lead through those conversations with influencers.

Keep in mind that scheduling influencers for these types of conversations are best handled by someone else, we'll share more on that later.

**Success Stories**

In this type of episode, we feature someone who has gone through our coaching, paid for consulting, bought our book and taken action, or used our creative services, and, most importantly, gotten the results we promise.

There are ways to leverage conversations with influencers and solo episodes to share success stories. But our primary success stories should always be conversations with the people we have served, sharing the results of our work together.

**Solo Episodes**

In this type of episode, we teach, train, and lead. We hit record and deliver a direct message to our audience.

No guests, no interviews, no distractions. Just talk straight to our Audience. Why are Solo Episodes so important?

Think about the structure of a local Christian church, in which one person leads a much larger group of people. Churches are great examples of real influence. Local churches are built around the Sunday sermon.

Solo Episodes are like our sermon to our church.

It's fine to have guest speakers a couple times a month; that's the purpose of Influencer Conversations.

But at least once a month, our audience needs to hear *us* delivering the message they need at that exact point to change. To grow. To transform. Cultivating new beliefs so they take new actions and get new results.

To deliver the right message, we must keep a pulse on our Audience. That means talking with them consistently—either on the phone, via social media or messaging apps, or at events. This is the only way to get the real-time feedback we need to deliver the right message.

One of the best examples of this real-time feedback and leadership is our client and podcast host Greg Harrelson, who leads a team of agents in real estate offices in the Carolinas, a team that sells well over 2,000 homes a year and generates millions in gross commissions.

Greg is in the office every day talking with his agents in person, plus he's talking to his podcast audience in Facebook Workplace and Messenger, where he encourages people to reach out with questions.

Through the conversations with his agents and his podcast Audience, he understands what people are struggling with in real time. At least once a week, he delivers a message to the agents in his office based on what he's hearing and seeing from them.

Then we help him take the most impactful of those messages and deliver that same content through Solo Episodes of his podcast.

In other words, he delivers a message to help his Audience grow. That's real leadership. That's why Solo Episodes are so critical to our Weekly Podcast Formula.

But why weekly? Couldn't we grow faster by producing more content?

Not necessarily. More content isn't always better.

There are numerous reports from podcast hosts I know personally where dropping the number of episodes they released actually improved their download numbers.

If we want to do more than a weekly episode, our recommendation is to record more Solo Episodes. Share our Point of View from different angles. Reinforce our beliefs with more stories, anecdotes and evidence. Drive home our Clear & Compelling Idea.

But ultimately, our podcast must be sustainable for us.

My business coach once said, "We should all aspire to do our best. But our best isn't the maximum we could push ourselves to do over the short term. Our best doesn't leave us burned out and exhausted. Our best is sustainable."

The same applies to podcasting.

Could we do three episodes a week? Of course. For a while.

At one point in my podcasting career I was recording four to six episodes a week with guests, plus Solo Episodes.

As a result, I built a huge backlog of episodes.

It was amazing for networking and relationship-building, but I burned out on it. It wasn't sustainable. And, therefore, it wasn't my best.

Whenever we catch ourselves thinking more content is always better, think again. More isn't automatically our best, especially when it's unsustainable.

By plugging into a Weekly Podcast Formula, we deliver the right content in a way that's sustainable for most us over the long term.

# Share Success Stories

What happens when everyone has credentials? A degree, a certification, a diploma, a seal of approval from some official organization?

More supply equals lower demand and lower value. Which means education credentials lose more value with each passing day.

As a result, we're seeing a massive shift. Education credentials no longer carry the same weight. Our audience is realizing that education credentials prove we can learn, yet they don't prove we can produce results for them.

How does this shift affect thought leaders?

As people become more skeptical and education credentials drop in value, our social credentials start to carry more weight. People are looking for more evidence from their peers, their colleagues, and our fellow thought leaders before they will pull the trigger.

To generate demand and create new ideal clients, we need more than just testimonials and reviews. We need success stories.

The right success story can ...

- inspire and stir up emotion
- reinforce beliefs
- motivate new action
- encourage the weary to continue
- deliver a well-timed kick in the pants
- create a shared connection

- raise social status
- build a sense of community

Success stories accomplish all this by delivering a clear and relatable vision of the results we promise, while reinforcing beliefs, building trust, and demonstrating leadership.

Success stories show our belief system in action. They are the real-world evidence of how new beliefs create new actions, and new actions create new results.

This evidence of success is a critical element in building the trust required to turn demand into sales. Every call to action we deliver can be more effective by pairing the call to action with a targeted success story.

In a sales situation, success stories can be the tiebreaker between multiple coaches or consultants. Success stories from influencers can carry even more weight and help prospective clients understand where we fit into the pecking order of our niche.

Yet success stories can also give an instant benefit, even when the results we promise take time to deliver. Through well-crafted success stories, we can tell the story that clients are doing more than signing up for a service—they're joining an elite group of like-minded people. That's an immediate boost in their social status— a very powerful strategy when we used authentically.

Because of all these benefits, success stories can improve every area of our business, from lead conversion and sales support all the way to client retention and past client reactivation.

We all agree that we need more success stories, yet we never seem to get around to it.

Here's the good news: our podcast solves that problem.

By featuring successful clients on our podcast, we generate a consistent stream of success stories that can be broken down into bite-size chunks.

The goal of these conversations is to dig into the client's story and extract the Hero's Journey. They've reached the Promised Land and are coming back to the wilderness to share their journey.

We want to highlight the new actions they took to create those new results and then tie those actions back to the tools and systems we teach.

By tying their actions to *our tools and systems*, instead of *us*, we avoid creating the wrong kind of demand. When we create demand that can only be filled by our time, effort, and energy, we risk locking ourselves into a business we hate.

Once we've highlighted our tools and systems, we can dig into the limiting beliefs they overcame, the new beliefs they adopted, and how those new beliefs supported their new actions. This helps convert our Audience to our beliefs, getting them moving in our direction, aligned and ready to take new action and get the results we promise.

What happens if we can't get successful clients to share their story publicly?

This is more common in consulting than coaching or creative work, yet it does come up for all of us sometimes. Sometimes this hesitation is linked to fear; the client is afraid that sharing their journey publicly will lower their social status. They may also fear that their competitors will hire us and go on to surpass their success.

There are many ways to get around this kind of fear, including keeping numbers and metrics vague, focusing on their hard work instead of our genius, or even signing non-disclosure agreements for specific facts they want to keep to themselves.

Yet our experience has shown that having a podcast prevents most of this reluctance. Being invited to appear on a podcast feels completely different from being asked to give a testimonial. Who doesn't enjoy sharing their success?

# Build One Great Social Platform

Before we show up on a social platform, it's helpful to ask, "Why are people showing up there? What are they expecting to get from that platform?"

This helps us step outside our goals, our metrics, and our place in the Battle.

Remember, we're not the only ones asking those questions. Social media companies ask these questions every single day. They want to keep people on their platform and engaging with other users.

As a result, social platforms are shifting to reward things like connection, conversation, and community.

This book proposes a very different approach to social media based around beliefs that are unpopular, yet drawn from solid evidence.


**Unpopular Belief #1: Social platforms are a reality bubble.**

In other words, every social platform forms its own ecosystem—complete with its own winners. That ecosystem is not directly connected to the real world of sales and market share.

This means that…

success on social media guarantees nothing in real life

success in real life guarantees nothing on social media

For thought leaders, this means it's possible to own the top social platform in our space without the real-world results to back it up. We can build the biggest online community or podcast in our space and still fail to generate demand or drive sales in the real world.

This leads us to the next unpopular belief.

**Unpopular Belief #2: Attention doesn't convert to sales automatically.**

If attention converted to sales, whoever owns the top social platform in a niche would own that niche in sales.

On the contrary, we can find many examples of thought leaders running the #1 business in a niche without owning any of the top social platforms.

Clearly, it's not a straight line from attention to sales.

**Unpopular Belief #3: The biggest winners on social media are those who get the timing right.**

After the fact, it's easy to attribute success to hard work and better tactics. Yet this ignores the biggest factor in the explosive growth of big winners—the growth of the social platform itself.

Over time, social platforms tend to follow the same pattern:

Early adopters work out the kinks while a platform is in its early days. The platform itself focuses relentlessly on acquiring new users, supported by venture capital that allows them to lose money on each new user.

As the social platform gets better at delivering a great user experience, the platform hits a tipping point and moves into a phase of explosive growth.

Some of these early adopters build large audiences as the platform goes through this explosive growth phase. As this happens, more people jump in, chasing the early adopters, without understanding the conditions that supported their growth.

Then the platform levels off as it matures, while the early adopters turn around and sell programs on how to duplicate their success.

As a result, other influencers and thought leaders jump in too late to catch the explosive growth phase, *but expect the same results and get frustrated in the process.* Then a new social platform comes out and the cycle starts all over again.

While there are lots of great tactics that can help us succeed on social media, it's important to remember that the biggest winners on social media get the timing right. Applying the same tactics while ignoring the timing is a recipe for frustration.

**Unpopular Belief #4: Social platforms always put the user over everyone else.**

This is exactly how social platforms generate explosive growth. If they don't put the user experience first, the platform doesn't grow. Simple as that. Business brands and thought leaders are always lower on the priority list.

In fact, in the world of social platforms, business brands and thought leaders are piggy banks. We are trying to reach new people with our message, so we buy ads. Users don't like ads, so it's a game to see how much advertising a social platform can handle without losing users. If the platform can keep up that game long enough, it can be acquired by a bigger company. This allows founders and investors to cash out before everyone else figures out the game and moves to a newer platform with less advertising.

Of course, the positive side is that if we learn to work *with* the social platform and give users what they want, the social platform will support us.

Yet we need to be aware of the final unpopular belief.

**Unpopular Belief #5: Social platforms are never truly free.**

First, our time, effort, and energy are not infinite. Which means every second of time and every ounce of energy and capital we invest into a social platform is time, energy, and capital not invested somewhere else. In other words, there is an opportunity cost to every social platform.

Second, most platforms eventually require thought leaders to pay to play. In the early days, thought leaders are allowed to play for free. We help fill the platform with content, which keeps users engaged and telling others about the platform. Then, at some point, we have to pay to reach the Audience we built.

When it comes to social platforms, free is not "zero-cost." Every platform is an investment of resources.

Based on these unpopular beliefs, here is the MicroFamous approach to social media.

Our goal is one great social platform...

...creating connection, conversation, and community

...while leading our Audience back to our podcast

...where we can share content that cultivates ideal clients

...so we can help solve their problem and deliver the results we promise.

Now let's dig into each of these elements.

**Build one great platform.**

We don't need to be omnipresent. That's a luxury for companies with big teams and big budgets.

For solo thought leaders or those with small teams, one great social platform with genuine conversations and community beats running a ghost town on every platform. Since our time, energy, and effort are limited, why not concentrate our resources where they can be the most effective?

**Create connection, conversation, and community.**

People use social platforms to connect with people, have conversations and feel a sense of community. The thought leaders who show up for the right reasons and help create connection, conversation, and community will win. Everyone else will struggle to gain traction.

**Lead people back to our podcast.**

Social platforms change daily, sometimes hourly. Why leave the relationship with our Audience to the whims of social platforms?

Our podcast is the place where people spend the most time with us, the place where we can draw people into a deeper relationship. It's our incubator of ideal clients.

That's why connection, conversation, and community are so important.

Without those elements on our social platform, people may consume our content yet never take a real step toward us.

So, how do we lead people from social media to our podcast?

We start by sharing micro-content pulled from our podcast.

Micro-content is a small, bite-sized chunk of content that conveys emotion, beliefs, and ideas that lead back to our podcast and support our Clear & Compelling Idea.

Then we follow up on that micro-content by engaging with people, creating connection, conversation, and community. We don't post and run, we post and engage.

This simple approach helps us understand where all social media platforms fit into our business, helping us avoid shiny object syndrome.

Now let's look at how to use micro-content to do more than engage our Audience on social platforms.

# Create Micro-Content that Converts

Sales is where leaders shine. If we can't convert attention and demand into real clients who get real results, what have we really accomplished?

But we've agreed that we don't want just *any* clients. We want ideal clients.

Clients who are already moving the same direction we are, clients who share our beliefs, clients who trust our leadership.

As we put our MicroFamous strategy into action, delivering the right content to the right people – *systematically* – we uncover a new challenge.

What content do we send people who raise their hand to express interest in working with us?

Raising their hand is a sign that they've entered a different phase. They are considering a client relationship, where they work with us to solve a real problem and get the results we promise. This is a much deeper level of connection and relationship, and therefore a much deeper level of commitment.

So we can't simply send them more of the same content.

Resistance naturally comes up at this point: objections, limiting beliefs, concerns, doubts, and fears. This is especially true when clients must take action to get the results we promise.

If we're good at selling ourselves, we'd love to show up and hold their hand through the sales process, delivering the right content at the right time to help them reach the best decision.

That's what great salespeople do—they help build great decisions.

Yet we already know that in the world of B2B sales, 60% of the sales process takes place before a prospect ever gets on a call with a salesperson. Then there's a portion of the sales process that takes place after a sales call. Therefore, we don't control the majority of the sales process, even if the product we're selling is *us*.

Prospects spend the majority of the sales process interacting with our content, not us.

They are off by themselves, weighing the price tag of our solution against the results we're promising, all the while dealing with internal resistance.

Which means we need content that addresses that resistance and helps them reach the right decision.

Content that...

- humanizes us and our brand
- builds trust and credibility
- supports good decision-making
- deals with fear and limiting beliefs
- sets good expectations

Since we can't hold our prospect's hand through most of this process, our next best option is to create bite-sized chunks of content that could take our place as a salesperson.

This might sound far-fetched, but it's really no different from the way an infomercial can take the place of a door-to-door salesperson.

Once we create the right content that helps prospects build a great decision, the goal is simply to put that content into their hands at the right time.

Of course, we could create all this content from scratch. However, a New Media Machine gives a better solution: repurpose, repackage and optimize content from our podcast into Sales Micro-Content.

A common example would be a highlight clip from a podcast episode. Excerpts from client testimonials and case studies or highlights of key interviews and guest appearances also make great bite-sized chunks.

For each objection, limiting belief, fear, misconception, or concern, we can create a piece of Sales Micro-Content that addresses and eliminates that resistance. This Micro-Content is pulled from podcasts and optimized for the sales process.

Once we have that stockpile of Sales Micro-Content, we can set our goals even higher. We can do more than just influence the sales process; we can create a sales system.

A system that delivers targeted Sales Micro-Content at the right time to the right people.

A system that converts prospects into new clients - predictably and consistently.

A system so good that even when a prospect decides not to move forward, they either feel like they're making a poor decision, or they aspire to work with us when they can afford us.

By mapping our Sales Micro-Content to respond to real objections, limiting beliefs, and resistance, and by building that Sales Micro-Content into a sales system, we take back control of the sales process.

# Don't Fight Alone

In a world where everyone is an influencer, we can't win the Battle for Attention alone. Everyone needs allies.

What do we mean by an ally in the Battle for Attention?

We've found three kinds of allies:

Assistants, Producers, and Experts.

*Assistants* handle the daily essentials. Pitching us on podcasts, scheduling interviews, creating graphics, posting content, editing audio and video for our podcast, and pulling out micro-content for social media and sales.

*Producers* handle the higher-level activities and keep our New Media Machine running smoothly. Their role is similar to an operations manager. They manage projects, build new systems, and improve existing systems. They also manage relationships with affiliates, strategic partners, outside experts, and agencies.

*Experts* are typically not on our team; rather, they help us in specific cases. They come in at the crucial times when we are setting or changing our strategy, systems, and tactics. They are masters of their craft who deliver critical information, guidance, or expertise.

Now that we see these kinds of allies, it becomes clear that doing everything ourselves is basically assigning ourselves to all three roles. What are the odds we're good at all three? Pretty slim.

So, where do we turn for allies in the Battle for Attention?

I believe we start with an Assistant first, then find a Producer, and work with Experts along the way as needed.

Here's how that process fits into the bigger picture.

First, we set our MicroFamous strategy, either by ourselves or with the help of an Expert. Our strategy lays out our path to become famously influential to the right people.

Once we have our strategy in place, we can build our New Media Machine, one stage at a time. We start by hiring an Assistant to pitch us as a guest on podcasts.

Our Assistant sets us free from routine tasks, allowing us to invest our time in our highest-value activities. These activities include recording podcast episodes, engaging with our Audience on social media, and closing sales.

This keeps clients coming in while we're also working behind the scenes on the operations of our business.

We may also find we need to work with an outside Expert to do something specific such as launch a podcast. If we have the resources and can handle the investment and time commitment, working with an Expert at this stage can be a huge win.

Here are four reason why our allies can make or break our MicroFamous strategy.

**Growth requires more time on high value activities.**

Getting personally involved in the daily essentials of our New Media Machine pulls us away from the highest-value activities that build real influence and attract ideal clients.

**Focus requires priorities.**

It's easy to overestimate our own bandwidth, thinking we have all the time and energy in the world to tinker with new ideas. A good Producer understands our MicroFamous strategy and often comes to know our capacity better than we do. They help us stay focused on the activities that support our strategy and put everything else on the back burner.

**Creativity requires space.**

If we're in the weeds all the time, it's hard to relax and be creative. As a result, we often miss opportunities. Our allies live in the weeds for us, running our New Media machine so we are free to think creatively, have more fun conversations, and take advantage of short-term opportunities.

**Results require customization.**

There are no silver bullet tactics that get the same results for everyone. It takes customization to produce the best results. Our allies help us customize the tactics of our New Media Machine to generate the best results.

Along the way we'll want to experiment with all kinds of things; the length of our podcast episodes, different types of videos and blog articles to publish, new forms of micro-content and a host of other elements. Nothing wrong with customization.

Yet an outside agency or freelancers can't deliver customization, quality AND consistency. It's just not sustainable.

That's why it's best to build a New Media Machine 'in-house.'

The more of our New Media machine is run by people who report to us directly, the more freedom we have to experiment and customize our content.

So, we start with an Assistant, progress to a Producer, and work with Experts along the way. The right allies in the right place at the right time.

# PART THREE
## TACTICS

# New Media Tactics in a MicroFamous World

This final section of the book is based on the most common questions that arise while building and running a New Media Machine in a thought leader business.

It's designed to be a quick reference guide, showing how specific tactics fit into the New Media Machine and support the MicroFamous strategy. We cover tactics from all four of the most effective forms of new media content: podcast interviews, podcast hosting, micro-content for sales, and micro-content for social media.

Remember, tactics should never drive strategy. When we stay focused and approach tactics last, we eliminate distraction and push forward...*systematically*.

# Get Featured on 50 Podcasts in the Next 12 Months

One interview a week is all it takes to do 50 podcasts in the next 12 months. Considering the average podcast episode gets 200 downloads, and 500 is pretty typical for a business podcast, that strategy will reach a minimum of 10,000 people.

Unlike video views or other types of engagement, where our "viewers" might just be scrolling past our content at breakneck speed, podcast interviews are long-form conversations where 80% of listeners consume all or most of each episode.

For thought leaders, there simply is no better opportunity in new media than podcast interviews. It's the #1 new media tactic we recommend to any influencer at any stage, and it's the first stage in our New Media Machine.

Given the power and effectiveness of podcast interviews, we don't want to leave podcast interviews to chance or occasional bursts of our personal effort.

We need a system that ensures that we get featured consistently, and that those episodes are shared and promoted to our Audience to get the maximum effect.

Our New Media Machine starts with a simple Podcast Pitch Assistant system, in which our Assistant...

- finds industry and niche business podcasts
- locates contact info for podcast hosts
- sends a well-crafted, professional pitch email that makes it easy for podcast hosts to say Yes!
- schedules podcast interviews in our calendar

- overcomes objections, communication, and tech issues in the booking process
- reports their progress and prepares us for each podcast interview

And all this happens in around two to three hours per week, while protecting our most important asset—our reputation.

When we get this system up and running, at first our Assistant will need to send about five pitch emails every week to get one booked. But that ratio improves quickly.

Success breeds success, and podcast interviews start to take on a life of their own. Bigger podcasts come calling, invitations start to roll in, our response rates go up, and we don't need to pitch ourselves as much to get one interview a week consistently and systematically.

Of course, we know what we're doing and how to present ourselves as a good guest. Couldn't we just pitch ourselves?

Absolutely, but we don't recommend it.

It's difficult for thought leaders to devote the time needed to pitch ourselves consistently, so the best we end up with is occasional and inconsistent bursts of pitching.

On top of that, our time is better spent being visible, closing new clients, and improving our operations. **The only part of a podcast interview we should be doing is the interview itself.** Let the Assistant handle the pitching, so we can do more income-generating activities.

What about hiring a PR firm?

Many experts and entrepreneurs have gone that route, including friends and clients. They often find that the benefit doesn't outweigh the cost and they have no control over what shows are being pitched.

So, they end up using a PR firm only for short bursts of three to six months. Having an Assistant pitch us consistently means we're getting featured week in and week out. It's consistent, scalable, sustainable, and 100% under our control.

What if we don't have time to be interviewed?

We all have times where we are immersed in a project or we want to be less visible. Yet even the busiest and most successful thought leaders usually make time for the right podcast interview. They set an example we can all follow. In times of looming project deadlines or lower visibility, we simply have our Assistant limit their pitches to large podcasts that would make a huge impact.

However, if our goal is to featured consistently, we shouldn't limit ourselves to just the top podcasts. We should be pitched consistently to small and medium podcasts as well.

Often, the larger the podcast, the longer it takes from pitch email to published episode. Larger podcasts also may not consider us a good fit until we have a track record of successful interviews on smaller shows. Podcast hosts have every right to screen their guests. After all, the hosts are trying to grow their podcast by featuring guests who bring amazing content or their own Audience.

Small- and medium-sized podcasts sometimes have the most engaged niche audiences. Which means they might actually generate *better* prospects and higher sales than one large podcast interview.

The more consistently we get featured, the longer the track record we build, and the more likely we are to get featured on a big podcast with a big audience.

When we get featured on podcast interviews, our goal is to deliver our Clear & Compelling Idea and get them to take action.

That means we don't need seventeen different calls to action.

We only need two.

First, we need a Primary Call to Action for our main service—this could be high-ticket coaching and consulting, group coaching programs, or online courses. A small slice of a podcast audience might be ideal clients right now, so let's offer them an immediate solution to their problem.

Yet most will not be ideal clients today, so we need a Secondary Call to Action, a way for like-minded people to get into our Audience, where we can incubate them to become ideal clients down the road. Free giveaways work well for Secondary Calls to Action, where we can solve some small, tactical problem that builds trust and authority.

Both Calls to Action must be clear and memorable to the *ear*, not just the eye. Podcast listeners are rarely sitting at their laptop, so there's no point in giving them a URL that looks good and sounds like gobbledygook.

We recommend setting up pretty links or custom domains that are verbally memorable. They should roll right off the tongue and be easily recalled minutes later. Stick to URL's that are clear, simple, and verbally memorable.

By giving two calls to action which are clear and memorable, we make it easy for listeners to take action, either to buy from us or give us permission to stay in touch.

This draws like-minded people into our Audience and builds a long-term asset—an email list of the right people who have given us permission to send them content on a regular basis.

With all the available tools and tactics, it's easy to forget that a permission-based email list is still one of the most valuable assets in a thought leader business.

Armed with these tactics, podcast interviews are much more than temporary bursts of visibility. They are the key to leveraging outside audiences, generating authentic word of mouth, and building a permission-based email list.

# How to Be a Dream Podcast Guest & Make Friends with Hosts

Let's say we're booked on an important podcast, with a host we respect. We want to make a great impression, maybe even build a real friendship.

How do we accomplish that on a podcast interview? How can we put our best foot forward and lay the foundation for a real relationship?

Here are the top three steps to be a dream podcast guest, based on experience on both sides of the podcast mic.


**Show up for the host and the Audience first.**

Think less about our own goals and more about the host. Why did they start their podcast? What are they selling, and what do they want their listeners to take away from the conversation?

It's great to show up prepared, with a topic and talking points, yet the podcast host might want to take the conversation in a different direction to suit their listeners.

Podcast hosts talk to a ton of people, so they rarely want a canned presentation, scripts, or rigid talking points. Focus on the host and their listeners, bring value first, and we'll always earn the host's respect.

**Show up prepared.**

We don't have to listen to ten episodes or do a ton of research. If we're having our Assistant pitch us and set up the interview, it's really simple to show up prepared.

Our Assistant needs to add three things to each podcast interview they schedule on our calendar:

Podcast host's bio

Description of the podcast

Topic or content the host wants us to cover

This includes any additional notes on the content or segments to be prepared for, such as "lightning rounds" or "best advice you've ever received."

With a good scheduling system, and a quick review of the calendar appointment before jumping on an interview, it's easy to be prepared.


**Show up with good audio and video.**

Several years ago, we booked a guest on a client's podcast.

The guest called into a video podcast recording session from a noisy gym, where he was in the middle of a workout. Needless to say, that guest was not rescheduled or booked on any of our other shows, and they may never know why.

That's an extreme example, but for busy thought leaders, it's easy to be some version of that person. Fortunately, it's not difficult or expensive to show up with good audio and video.

First, we need a high-quality microphone that picks up very little background noise.

We recommend the Audio-Technica ATR2100, specifically because it's *not* intended for recording studio environments.

Which means it doesn't need to live in an NPR studio to sound good. It sounds as good in a hotel room or a car as it does from a home office. And yes, one of our clients has done podcast episodes from a car with this microphone and they turn out great.

Yet even once we have a good setup at home, our schedule can still trip us up. To prevent this, we can review a few key things each morning as we look over our calendar and visualize the day.

What appointments are best done from our home office?

What do we need to do today to make sure we show up on time and prepared?

What's our backup plan if we can't be at our home office for some reason?

Running quickly through those three questions each morning helps prevent us from being the annoying podcast guest who shows up with poor audio or video.

These steps are simple and easy, which is exactly why so many podcast guests neglect them. Yet they go a long way toward starting a real relationship with the podcast host, which can generate benefits for years or decades.

# Podcasting is the New Networking

As it becomes more expensive and time-consuming to reach new people online, every thought leader needs a network of key relationships with fellow thought leaders.

These are the people who can send us referrals, introduce us to key people, feature us on their podcasts, promote us to their email list, share resources, and split lead generation costs to reach new people.

To build a network of strategic relationships, it's best to start conversations in a way that puts us on equal footing. We all want to build relationships with others at our level of influence or higher.

**In other words, leaders want to network with other leaders.**

We've found that the most powerful way to start a conversation with a thought leader is by introduction from someone they trust and respect.

Doors that are shut tight and bolted down can fly open with the right introduction. This applies both in person and online. The challenge is that personal networking is time-consuming, expensive, and unscalable; it involves lots of flights, drinks, and hotels.

Fortunately, podcasting has given us better options for scaling up introductions and building a network of key relationships.

In other words, podcasting is the new networking.

Podcasting has some very powerful advantages over other forms of networking. Let's cover a few of the most basic, along with ways to leverage these tactics.

**Trusted Introductions**

Podcasting gives thought leaders and influencers a valid reason to introduce each other. I can't count the number of introductions that only happened because one (or both) of the people being introduced hosted a podcast.

It's one of the best networking strategies I've personally found, not just for the people being introduced, but for the person making the introduction. When that introduction goes well, all the good feelings that come from that new relationship gets linked to the person who made the introduction.

**Peer Status**

Podcasting can substitute for a trusted introduction because it puts thought leaders on more equal footing. We have peer status because we're all part of the same club.

Right now, thought leaders and influencers understand the value of building relationships, so we *want* to connect with other thought leaders on podcasts. It's become one of the easiest ways to start a conversation in the world of thought leaders and influencers.

**Authentic Name Dropping**

By referencing mutual friends and connections when we reach out, we generate some of the power of a trusted introduction.

It shows that not only are we peers in general, but we run in the same *circles*. Every podcast conversation is an opportunity to expand our network of relationships.

I use this tactic in virtually every new conversation with a podcast host, putting in the work to identify the friendships and relationships we might have in common. If I can find an authentic connection or mutual friend, I immediately build connection and credibility.

## Time & Trust

Once we've started a conversation, the depth and length of the conversation plays a big role in how fast the new relationship develops. This is where podcasting really shines.

Because conversations are typically 30 to 60 minutes, podcasting allows us to spend more time with the host than we would typically get in other forms of conversation. The connection and bond is often stronger than meeting in person because we can get into deeper, longer conversations with fewer distractions.

Every podcast host is a doorway to other thought leaders, other audiences, and other relationships. So, every podcast interview is an opportunity to build our network of key relationships.

The more we focus on building those relationships, the more we'll find ways to leverage podcasting as the new networking.

# Accelerate New Relationships – Systematically

If podcasting is the new networking, how do we step on the gas pedal and accelerate new relationships?

Through our podcast interviews, we're being consistently introduced to new influencers and thought leaders. How do we get maximum value from those conversations?

Fortunately, it's the simple things that can turn one conversation into a series of conversations. In fact, thanks to new tools and social platforms, there are lots of relationship-building activities to choose from.

However, rather than add all these activities to a To Do list and attack it with brute force, the goal is to build a *Relationship-Building System* where most of these activities take place behind the scenes.

We simply the trigger the system once and provide the information our Assistant needs to execute it.

Relationship-building activities fall into two general categories: *high-tech* and *high-touch*. High-tech involves apps, software, and online tools and services, and tends to be the easiest to automate and delegate. High-touch is much more personal, time-intensive, and customized, making it more difficult to automate and delegate. Let's look at a few of the proven options for each category.

## High-Tech

*Add every new connection to our CRM*—We can take this a step further by marking the relationships that are worthy of more attention and focus.

One of the best methods we've found is to create a New Connection Email Template, which can be filled out during a call or podcast. The email template helps us jot down all the relevant information, and then send the completed email to an Assistant who handles the data entry. A New Connection Email Template can be saved as a Canned Response in Gmail.

With the right CRM, we could also trigger a follow-up series of emails that offers other ways to connect, such as an online community or affiliate network.

*Connect on LinkedIn*—This continues to build our network, making it easier to reach out to other thought leaders and ideal clients on LinkedIn. Once we're connected, it opens other avenues for high-touch communication, like LinkedIn recommendations and endorsements.

The more high-value connections we have on LinkedIn, the easier it is to reach out to new people and drop names in an authentic way. Adding new connections and sending a follow-up thank you message is easily delegated to our Assistant.

*Connect on social platforms*—This makes us more human and potentially uncovers shared interests, hobbies and passions.

*Add new connections to our primary email list (with real permission)*—This ensures they're expecting to receive our best content and gives them a reason to reach out when they spot an interesting message.

We always want to add like-minded people to our email list with a high degree of permission, so that we have more of the right people looking forward to our content. Focus on the right people, not just more people.

These are all actions that can be taken on primarily by our Assistant with very simple tools like templates, training videos and checklists.

Now let's look at the high-touch activities.

**High-Touch**

*Send Thank You Cards*—I love sending personalized thank you cards, and handwriting them ourselves is the ultimate high-touch activity.

For those who have near-illegible handwriting (like me), there are companies like SendOutCards that make it easy to streamline this process. We can even get our Assistant involved by having them transcribe our thank you message and ordering the card.

There are also tools and services that can mimic human handwriting, or even services where actual human beings handwrite the notes for you. Either way, as the world goes more digital, thank you notes stand out even more.

*Send books*—This is a great way to show we were truly paying attention during conversations with other influencers. As an avid reader, I often think of relevant books during these conversations, and it's a great opportunity to send a key book and accelerate the relationship.

My favorite example is with my good friend and mentor Pat Scopelliti (the strongest advisor for business leaders you will ever find).

I first talked to Pat while booking him as a podcast guest and we had a great conversation. Several days later, a book shows up in the mail. Attached is a note from Pat explaining how much he loved the book and where it might be helpful in my business.

Not only was the gesture thoughtful and impactful, I devoured the book and followed up with Pat to share how much I enjoyed it. That conversation led first to a friendship, then to an official coaching relationship. All from one high-touch action that accelerated our relationship.

Amazon makes it easy to order books and send a personal note, or we can keep certain books on hand and write personal notes on the first page. If we've written our own book, having our Assistant send a copy with a personal note inside is another great option.

*Look for introduction opportunities*— Essentially, we look for opportunities to be a connector by introducing influential people to each other. This is the best strategy I've found for accelerating relationships. In the world of influencers and thought leaders, introductions are a form of relationship currency. The more strategic the introduction we can make, the higher the impact.

*Strategic endorsements and recommendations on LinkedIn*—Few people use LinkedIn strategically, so endorsements and recommendations on the platform are high-impact compared to the time it takes to give them.

Not only are they genuinely valuable to the other person (who can use them in all their marketing and sales support material), but people who receive them are also likely to return the favor.

*Promote older content featuring key influencers*—Most of us are terrible at promoting older content, so sharing older podcast episodes featuring a key influencer, tagging them if possible, is a great touch point and helps strengthen the relationship.

When it comes to relationships, we all have good intentions.

Yet for most of us, our business takes up a great deal of our emotional and mental horsepower.

Building relationships requires mental and emotional space. Space to be thoughtful. Space to uncover opportunities. Space to care about others more than ourselves. That space shrinks when we're under stress, effectively putting blinders on us.

Because I've tracked the numbers, I've noticed a direct link between stress and relationship-building actions like introductions. Higher stress = fewer introductions made.

Whenever I would see a drop in the number of introductions I was making, I found a direct tie to higher stress levels. It was in those times of stress that I neglected our Relationship Building System the most.

The best way to get started is to begin with a few key actions that are authentic to us, document how we want them done, and get our Assistant involved to help.

Don't leave relationship-building to chance. Turn it into a system. A Relationship-Building System doesn't make our activities any less authentic; our system just ensures that we follow through on our good intentions.

# 5 Tactics to Get Podcast Hosts Coming to Us

Once we start getting featured consistently, success breeds success. Podcast invitations start to come into us, as well as invitations to appear on live stages, webinars, virtual summits, and video series.

However, I've stumbled into some tactics that can accelerate this attraction process and generate podcast invitations, without pitching ourselves directly.

Here are a few things to keep in mind about these tactics.

They are not a substitute for our Assistant pitching us consistently.

They are indirect and can take longer to produce results.

They are a great way to build Authority, Visibility & Relationships in their own right.

We may not have all of these listed assets we can leverage right away, such as a book or current relationships with trade publications, yet knowing that these tactics are available can open our minds and help us spot new opportunities.

## LinkedIn Outreach

Right now, LinkedIn is still the most undervalued social platform among thought leaders. There's so much potential for genuine connection and conversation, yet that potential is already drawing in bad actors using virtual assistants and automation tools to spam people with canned messages. If that trend continues, LinkedIn may lose its effectiveness as a platform to connect with other thought leaders. So let's maximize it while we can.

Start with a simple search for podcast hosts in our industry or niche. Often, these are thought leaders like business coaches, consultants, authors, speakers and trainers. Send a connect request with a short message.

Here's an example:

*Hey, NAME! Saw that we're connected through John Smith and Sally Jones, I was a guest on Sally's podcast last week. Looks like we run in similar circles, so let me know if there's anyone I can introduce you to! - Matt*

A simple message like this can kick off great conversations that turn into connect calls and podcast interview invitations. The key is to be sincere, be conversational, and look for ways to be genuinely helpful. Super long, formal messages will probably get ignored, so the more personal and human the better.

Some LinkedIn users check to see who viewed their profile on a regular basis. Sometimes just viewing the profiles of podcasts hosts, with no connect request, can be enough for the host to reach back out and start a conversation. We can encourage this to happen more often by optimizing our LinkedIn profile and regularly searching for podcast hosts to connect with on the platform.

**Offer a Strategic Introduction**

Reach out to podcast hosts and offer to connect them with a specific person from your network who might be an ideal guest. As opposed to a general offer, this is a very specific offer to make one high-value, strategic introduction.

If the podcast host agrees to the introduction, follow up with an enthusiastic introduction that complements both sides and explains why we believe they should meet.

125

Here's an example:

*Hey John and Sally! I came across Sally through a mutual friend and immediately thought she'd be a great guest for John's podcast. I think her background and topic would be a perfect fit, and hopefully it's just a good connection for both of you. I'll let you two take it from here, and let me know if there's anything more I can do to help! - Matt*

Often in the process, the host will want to know more about us and can lead to an invitation for us to appear on the podcast as well.

A great little side-version of this tactic is to systematically pitch our own happy clients to podcast hosts as potential guests. Those happy clients are going to have good things to say about us when they're interviewed.

## Write for Trade Publications

This includes both online and off. Once we're approved as a contributor and begin to write feature articles, blog posts, reports, editorials, or curated lists, we'll start to attract more podcast opportunities.

Podcast hosts either see our articles directly, or they see us on articles that list the major influencers in our space, and reach out to us. Those types of articles are frequently written by the major trade publications, who like to promote their own contributors as influencers.

We can also combine this strategy with direct outreach. By leveraging the mutual "club" we belong to as contributors, it gives us a clear reason to reach out to every other contributor and introduce ourselves.

The top of every niche is a very small world, with a tangled web of mutual benefit relationships, joint ventures, and back-scratching. This is not a criticism; most of it is completely natural and done with good intentions.

Becoming a trade publication contributor not only gives us a measure of credibility that often dwarfs the work involved, but also gives us access to that tangled web of influential relationships. Those relationships can be leveraged in many different ways to grow our influence. Invitations to appear as a podcast guest are just one of the most obvious.

**Write and Promote Our Book**

I've interviewed many, *many* business book authors, and almost all of them say the same two things:

1) It was far easier to get featured on podcasts once they had the clout of being an author, and...

2) Podcast interviews were the most effective strategy to actually sell the books.

Craig Ballantyne is a great example. To promote *The Perfect Day Formula,* he appeared as a guest on 275 podcasts, which he described as his most effective marketing strategy. The result was 30,000 sales of his book and 5,000 sales of his Perfect Day Formula Kit, an upsell to the book. (Side note, Craig shared this story on my podcast, where I interviewed him to feature and promote his book).

I recommend almost all my clients turn their attention to writing a book at some point, and the ability to leverage a book into podcast appearances is just one of the many benefits.

**Get Featured on Niche Podcasts**

This one seems obvious, so we have to dig a little deeper. Most podcast hosts are well-connected to other podcast hosts, and we often keep an eye on each other's podcasts and recent guests.

It's common for podcast hosts to introduce good guests to each other behind the scenes, or for one podcast host to hear a good guest and reach out to the host and request an introduction.

So, the more we get featured, and the more relationships we build with fellow thought leaders and podcast hosts, the more invitations we'll attract without our Assistant pitching us directly.

Remember, these are indirect tactics that take time to produce big results, so consistency is key. Our New Media Machine lays the foundation of systematic, consistent action, and then we have the option of leveraging some of these indirect tactics on top of that foundation.

# PODCASTS

VS

**Speaking
Engagements**

**The
Future**

**Writing
a Book**

**Traditional
Media**

# Podcasts vs Traditional Media

Think of traditional media coverage as short-form content delivered in a high-pressure situation.

Business podcasts are typically the opposite: long-form content in low-pressure situations.

The strength and potential of traditional media is its ability to reach a general, diverse audience. For thought leaders, this is also its greatest weakness. Traditional media is not built for small, lucrative niches. So we must be strategic in how we leverage traditional media.

When we look at thought leaders who get traditional media coverage, we often find they got their start by helping reporters and producers.

They spent months and years working their way up, pitching stories and segment ideas, being available on short notice and covering any topic that got them on-air experience.

It takes time to get a foot in the door, and every scrap of experience is hard to come by at that level. Some even take media training with former media pros just to handle those high-pressure situations.

In the podcast world, where the barrier to entry for guests is much lower, and there is a world of great options for getting featured, these tactics usually aren't necessary.

**In fact, applying these same traditional media tactics to podcasting can be counterproductive.** We can end up getting featured all over the place and yet creating zero demand and generating zero new business.

How can this be? Because when we take any opportunity that comes our way, we often have to cover topics that don't serve us.

Topics that don't connect to our Clear & Compelling Idea don't allow us to share our Point of View and don't relate to the problem we solve. All of which does nothing to create demand for us and our service.

In the world of MicroFamous, we build a New Media Machine first. Then, we can leverage traditional media to serve a few specific purposes:

**Authority**—Features in traditional media are great credibility indicators, especially to people outside our Audience or just coming into our Audience for the first time.

Best of all, we can leverage one appearance in many different ways for many years. Including a "Featured On" section of our website, future media pitches, our sales support system, and our nurture email campaign, we can reference just a few key appearances whenever we need authority.

**Expansion**—While traditional media is not built for small, lucrative niches, if we choose to expand into a larger niche, traditional media might be perfect.

When we uncover a Clear & Compelling Idea that has mainstream appeal, traditional media can be help launch us to a mainstream audience.

To maximize our traditional media opportunities, we must be able to move people into our Audience, earning their permission to stay in touch. That means promoting our podcast or email opt-in and adding those new people to our email list.

Otherwise, we run the risk of reaching a large audience and watching them slip through our fingers.

**Engagement**—Much like hit songs, people love a new twist on the familiar. Sharing our appearances on traditional media with our existing Audience puts a new twist on the familiar, showing us in new settings and environments.

This can be especially effective when those appearances pair us with traditional media influencers with whom our Audience is familiar. An audience loves to see their leader validated in public by other influencers; it reinforces their good decisions and creates buzz.

Traditional media has incredible—even life-changing—potential, *if* we have the right foundation and strategy in place.

However, because traditional media is not built for small, lucrative niches, it's critical for thought leaders to have a New Media Machine in place first. Only then can we bring people into our Audience and keep in touch with them consistently, leading them to new beliefs, new actions and new results.

# Podcasts vs Speaking Engagements

Most thought leaders I know can generate demand and close deals from live speaking engagements. So it's often one of the first tactics thought leaders try to scale up.

How do podcasts compare? Let's look at a common scenario.

You've been invited to come speak at an event, where you'll be put in front of a targeted audience of 200 people—at zero expense. Would you accept the invitation?

Most thought leaders I know wouldn't hesitate to say Yes.

Did you know the average podcast episodes gets 200 downloads?

That holds true even when we consider that about half of the 700,000 shows on Apple Podcasts right now are 6 months old or *less*. So if we accepted every invitation to appear as a podcast guest, on average, we're going to reach 200 people every time we get featured.

But to reach those 200 people, we didn't have to...

- negotiate fees
- deal with event logistics
- customize a talk for that audience
- set up all the travel

That's just the advance work. Then we have to actually do the traveling, which counts even if it's a "local gig." In major cities like LA or San Francisco, a local gig can still take up an entire day when we take traffic into consideration.

Then there's the extra, unforeseen obligations that often come with speaking gigs. The cocktail hours, award ceremonies, pictures, meet-and-greets, dinners, and so on. It's never just a speaking gig. There seems to always be some extra obligation that comes up.

That's not counting the opportunity cost of all the things we could have been doing in our business in all that time, and the energy drain of the travel—mentally, emotionally, and physically.

And yet I hear so many thought leaders asking more about getting more speaking gigs than about getting featured on more podcasts.

To reach the same 200 people on a podcast, we can do an interview which requires...

- little to no advance preparation
- zero travel
- 30 seconds to double-check the logistics
- no extra, unforeseen obligations
- no added opportunity cost

Not only that, but let's look at what happens when we speak at an event versus when we're getting featured on a podcast.

Typically, when we speak at an event, the Emcees are...not great. It's rare to be introduced by a high-level influencer, especially at smaller events. At best, they're a paid Emcee; at worst, they're an underling or team member assigned to introduce guest speakers.

They butcher our name, they can't read our bio correctly to save their life, and they have very little trust or authority built up with the audience. Whatever good things they say about us roll off people's backs.

Contrast that with a podcast hosted by a respected influencer, who has put thousands of hours into building their podcast, publishing quality content, and building trust and authority with their audience.

They introduce us as a trusted expert in our space, and the introduction positions us at a much higher level, allowing us to borrow much more of that trust they have built with the audience.

So even if we reach the *same exact 200 people*, I think we can agree that reaching them on a podcast is more effective and efficient than a speaking gig.

Now let's push this a step further.

Because the nature of podcasting allows for much smaller shows with more targeted audiences, the odds are good that if we're speaking to 200 people on a podcast, they're much more targeted than speaking to 200 people at an event.

That said, speaking gigs definitely have their place in our MicroFamous strategy and can be a great addition to our business when used in two very different ways:

**Occasional, strategic events**

We cherry pick and accept the events that have a high value for the relationships, authority, or other strategic reasons, and we keep the number very limited.

I accepted my first invitation to speak in Australia for both the relationship with the event organizer, but also so I could "check the box" and add international speaker to my resume. For me, that speaking event had high strategic value.

On the other end of the spectrum, we have...

## Consistent, scalable events

One of my clients uses events as the primary lead-generation activity in the business. As a result, she is on the road many, many days of the year. She and her team invest huge amounts of time, energy, and capital in the expectation that the leads generated by those events convert into coaching clients.

*The biggest pitfall here is to get caught in the middle of these two extremes.* Where we justify speaking gigs in the hopes of exposure and visibility, yet the events are not frequent or strategic enough to produce consistent results.

So, before we accept another speaking gig, let's ask ourselves a simple question: *How could we reach the same number of people through podcasts?*

# Podcasts vs Writing a Book

If we're asking this question, we're probably convinced that writing and publishing a book can build authority, create demand for our service, and give us access to more media outlets.

We might even entertain some idea of generating income from our book.

If we're considering writing a book or starting a podcast, let's go through the options so we can make the best decision.

First, let's look at some key points on books:

**Books are a one-time communication platform**

In other words, there is no *ongoing* communication with readers; our content is packaged into a form they can consume at their own pace. To have an ongoing impact, books must be leveraged with some other form of ongoing communication like a podcast.

**Books are not a key profit source for the vast majority of business authors**

This is something most of us don't find out unless we've talked to lots of thought leaders who have written and published books, ranging from self-publishing to full traditional publishing.

This isn't to say that books don't generate income, but rather that books are better at creating demand for professional services than generating income from book sales.

**Books don't sell themselves; they need to be pushed**

That applies even for books published through major traditional publishers. The biggest complaint I've heard from authors who went with a traditional publishing company is "My publisher did little or nothing to promote my book."

Sometimes the publisher didn't even follow through on the distribution in mainstream bookstores that the author was promised. For those who did get wide distribution, it didn't automatically transfer to sales. So let's take all that into consideration.

**Here are the strategic options to incorporate a book into our MicroFamous strategy.**

**Option 1: Book First**

Write our book and then leverage the book to get featured on podcast interviews before we launch our own podcast.

This option is best when we don't have clarity on our Point of View, who we serve, or how we're going to package and sell our services.

Dana Malstaff followed this path with Boss Mom® and it worked to perfection. She self-published and released her first book, then immediately hired a part-time

Assistant to pitch her as a podcast guest. Later, she launched her Boss Mom community on Facebook and the Boss Mom Podcast, which both exploded.

Writing the Boss Mom book first helped clarify her thinking, uncover her Clear & Compelling Idea, and identify her ideal client—the women she then attracted into her Facebook community. The Point of View she crafted in the writing process made her an attractive podcast guest, which made it easier to get featured. In turn, getting featured consistently built her email list and fueled the launch of her own podcast to a group of eager listeners.

This path isn't perfect, because it's possible to get bogged down in the writing process to the point of never actually releasing the book. Yet if we don't have our Point of View nailed down, writing our book first may be the best path.

## Option 2: Podcast First

Launch a podcast and build an Audience, then leverage our Audience as early adopters and advocates for the book.

This is what my friend Jay Campbell did, launching his podcast where he could nurture his social media following and build a community around his ideas. Jay was already clear on his Point of View. In fact, he had so much content and so many relationships with potential guests that hosting a podcast was far easier than writing a book.

Once the Audience was built up, Jay started writing and releasing books, leveraging the podcast audience and his email list to get over 200 five-star reviews for his books on Amazon. All these efforts drove more sales and more credibility while creating demand for each new book.

If we have clarity on our Point of View, our ideal client, and how we're going to package and sell our services, launching a podcast is a much faster, easier way to start building our Audience and cultivating ideal clients.

## Option 3: Launch Both

Launching a podcast and book at the same time is the hardest and most stressful to coordinate, yet if our goal is to launch a cohesive new brand into the market in a powerful way, it may be the right option.

This strategy works best when we have clarity on our Point of View, our ideal client, and how we package and sell our services, *and* we have an engaged, permission-based email list (the larger the better).

Social capital is limited, and social capital is what we cash in when we ask people to share our podcast or review our book. Promoting two different things splits our social capital in half.

Every time we ask for a book review, that's a podcast review we can't ask for. Every time we send people to our podcast, that's a call to action that isn't sending people to our book.

While it's a powerful strategy, I don't recommend it in most cases, because launching each one separately gives us the ability to focus our social capital on one launch at a time.

Finally, let's deal with a common trap in the book-writing process and how to avoid it. I call it the Hermit Genius Trap.

I have a lot of colleagues and friends in the business book publishing space.

And almost all of them point to a common mistake, especially with first-time authors.

The trap is writing and creating the book in secrecy—without real-time feedback along the way from our ideal audience.

It's tempting to write the content, pick the title, subtitle, and cover art we like the best, and put it into the world.

But without real-time feedback from our ideal audience, how do we know what resonates with them?

How do we know that our book is built around a Clear & Compelling Idea that resonates with them?

How do we build a group of advocates and champions who will help promote our book if the first they hear about it is when we're launching?

For those reasons and many more, I advise everyone in my world (and I'm taking this advice myself) to start by getting featured on podcasts first.

This path gives us some key benefits as we…

watch what resonates with podcast hosts and listeners.

build an engaged email list.

share the book writing process with our Audience and get the feedback we need to write the best possible book.

Before we lock ourselves away to write our masterpiece, consider these different paths and the Hermit Genius Trap.

Let's get featured on podcasts consistently and test and refine our ideas and concepts while we build a network of advocates who are looking forward to our book launch.

# Podcasts vs the Future

What happens as podcasting evolves and changes? We must remember that podcasting is just one way our audience can get new media content. It's a form of distribution.

I've always believed podcasting will evolve and the term "podcast" will probably go away; it's just a matter of time. Who remembers that the term "podcast" came from the iPod? As a new media platform, podcasts themselves might decline in popularity or get disrupted by the latest, greatest form of content.

Yet for thought leaders, the need for branded, long-form content will never go away. For now, we call this a podcast. That may change at some point.

Regardless of the term, thought leaders will always need a central place for branded, long-form video content—either live or pre-recorded. A place where people can consume 20, 30, or 40 minutes of content, spending large chunks of time with us. A primary place to attract an audience of like-minded people we can cultivate into ideal clients.

That's why we encourage all our podcast launch clients to record their episodes on video right away.

This gives the most flexibility when turning that long-form content into micro-content. Long-form video can easily be edited down into bite-size chunks, highlight clips, micro-content for social media, micro-content for sales, and much more.

For a podcast to be sustainable and effective over the long term, it must have 3 elements:

Control

Customization

Calls to Action

We must be able to experiment with elements like the content, the guests, how often we release new episodes, and the calls to action we promote.

As new social platforms and online media emerge in the future, we need a long-term platform we control that caters to our personality and preferences and gives us control of the critical elements.

Whether podcasting evolves slowly or gets disrupted overnight, we will always need a primary platform based on long-form video content to attract an Audience of like-minded people. A place where we lead people to new beliefs, new actions and new results.

# How to Know When It's Time to Launch a Podcast

As podcasting has exploded, it's easy to look at others who are having great success with podcasting and wonder if we should jump in.

To make a podcast the most effective and productive it can be for a thought leader, here are five questions we should ask ourselves. If we're unsure, or can honestly say No to several of these, it may be best to keep a podcast on the back burner. Let's look at each one.

*Are we getting featured on podcast interviews consistently?*

This matters because it's the fastest and most direct path to leverage podcasting.

Getting featured on other podcasts is a much lower barrier to entry and can be scaled up or down depending on the demands of our business.

It also gives us an inside look at the level of commitment and dedication it takes to run a podcast, by connecting with podcast hosts and seeing their process. Getting featured gives us an inside peek at how different hosts run their podcasts. (When you have to fill out a twenty-question form before being a guest, you'll think twice about asking your guests to do the same).

By getting featured, it sets a firm foundation to launch our own podcast. If we aren't already getting featured consistently, we need to get that stage of our New Media Machine running first.

*Are we getting requests to start a podcast—especially from people who have heard us on other podcasts?*

If we are visible online or getting featured consistently on podcasts as a guest, and people aren't asking us to start our own podcast, that might be an indication that something is missing.

That's why it's critical to ask ourselves these questions before launching a podcast. They can help us recognize some simple changes we can make, or skills we can build, to connect with audiences better before starting our own podcast.

*Are we searching for a way to authentically serve our audience—by leading them to better results even if they don't hire us?*

Podcasting is an ideal platform for leading an Audience. If we have something to say, not just something to sell, starting a podcast can be a great fit. By delivering our message straight to our Audience, we can convert them to our beliefs and make an impact on them long term.

What would happen if our Audience never bought from us, but they got amazing results from simply listening and taking action...would we want to continue the podcast? If we can honestly say yes, a podcast can be a great next step.

*Are we prepared to deliver content consistently and methodically build an Audience over 12 to 18 months?*

Podcasting is a media platform, and like any other platform, it takes time to attract an Audience. Some of the big names who have made a splash in podcasting over the last few years showed up with an established brand and a large, engaged email list. We should never set our expectations based on their success, because they're not actually starting from scratch.

If we're still in the early stages of building an Audience and an email list, podcasting won't magically build a massive audience or email list in a short time just because podcasting is trending.

Hosting a podcast is more than just an investment of time and money; it's an investment of energy. If our podcast doesn't give us back more energy than it takes along the way, we may quit before getting real traction.

We need to make sure our podcast will give us energy back by enjoying podcasting for its own sake. That way we can be consistent for the 12 to 18 months it takes to methodically build our Audience.

*Are we sold on the value of building relationships with influencers, and are we ready to capitalize on those opportunities?*

I recommend using the first 12 months of a podcast to build a network of strategic partners, fellow influencers and thought leaders who can send us clients directly, or refer us publicly.

Once those relationships are started through podcast conversations, we can take them offline into phone calls, meet-ups at events and conferences, speaking gigs, and much more.

Taking those relationships from podcast conversations to real life is the key, and can lead to a consistent stream of referrals for years or decades. Business is about relationships, even in the online world. That's the real power of hosting a podcast where we feature conversations with influencers on a regular basis.

If we can honestly answer YES to all five questions, we're in the perfect position to launch a podcast and capitalize on all the benefits of launching a podcast.

# Live vs Recorded Podcasts

I started my first podcast as a live Google Hangout series on YouTube months before we turned it into a podcast. Live video on YouTube, and later Facebook, was a huge contributor to the eventual success of the podcast.

So, live video remains one of my favorite forms of new media, and it can be the basis of a powerful podcast under the right conditions.

Yet live video also has some real drawbacks and isn't right for everyone. ***Pre-recording*—recording episodes behind the scenes—is still the dominant form of podcasting,** and I don't see that changing any time soon.

We'll start by laying out the benefits I personally experienced with live video, then we'll look at the drawbacks of live video and key elements to consider when choosing between live and pre-recorded video for a podcast.

**Benefits of Live Video:**

*Higher Engagement:* The ability to chat directly with our Audience during a podcast gives them a greater sense of community and connection. Especially when we can answer their questions or respond to their comments live and create inside jokes, running gags, and catch phrases.

One of the best parts of podcasting is having listeners reach out via private message or at events and start off with an inside joke from the podcast. It shows how much they listen and appreciate the content, which helps fuel the fire to keep podcasting.

*Higher Reach:* Since social platforms want to hold attention as long as possible, they have pushed live video over other forms of content. Which can mean reaching people we wouldn't have reached otherwise.

Yet there's a caveat—social platforms may not favor long-form content like live podcasts. We've already seen platforms shift to push short-form videos over long-form videos, and that doesn't account for future shifts away from newsfeeds to more groups and messaging.

So, we must make sure this element doesn't weigh too heavily in our decision. A live video show must be built that way for the long run, not for temporary boosts from social platforms.

*Higher Energy:* Whether it's the host or a guest, it seems that when everyone knows the podcast is on live video, everyone is a little more "on." We tend to raise our energy level and amplify our personality when we know a live audience is watching.

It's also exciting for guests to answer questions live and on the spot, giving them a chance to flex their muscles, demonstrate their expertise, and take the podcast in new and interesting directions. All this contributes to a more spontaneous feel that can be borderline addictive.

*Double the Promotional Potential:* With a live video show, we have two opportunities to promote the same content—first, we can promote the live broadcast in advance. Advance promotion can be as simple as a social media post or invitation to watch or a full-blown campaign with email and social media.

Then we can promote the edited "final" version when it's released to platforms like Apple Podcasts or published on our website. One piece of content, two opportunities for promotion.

*Real-Time Feedback:* This was one of my personal favorite aspects, and I feel like it made me a much better podcast host. By watching the viewer counts and comments in real time, I built a better sense of timing and learned how to better hold our Audience's attention.

I also made structural changes as a result of doing live video, which carried over into pre-recorded podcasts as well. After a lot of experimentation, I learned to hook an audience with small chunks of tactical content before diving into bigger questions, like a guest's background. That was a direct result of watching audience numbers in real time. But all these benefits come at a cost, so let's look at those next so we're equipped to make a great decision.

**Drawbacks of Live Video:**

*More Demanding:* Live video has more variables, including the technical aspects, the live audience, and the guest and their performance. The pressure to start and end the show on time makes smaller issues bigger than they would be otherwise.

To get all the benefits of live video, we must become comfortable speaking off the cuff, filling time, handling feedback from the audience, and making adjustments quickly and calmly. Because of all this, live video is simply more mentally and emotionally demanding, especially at first.

*More Audio/Video Issues:* Live video puts more pressure on every aspect of the technology chain, from the internet connection to integrations and applications that send our live video into a social platform.

Any issues that come up during a live broadcast must be dealt with on the fly, which sometimes means chatting through text with a guest while keeping the show going live and talking to fill time. That's a skillset that can be built, yet it doesn't come overnight.

*Less Editing Control:* Because everything is done on the fly on live video, and issues that come up are often referred to at other points of the show, it can take some creative editing to get the highest-quality final episode.

When there are audio/video issues, we have to decide to either cut out those portions, or simply live with a podcast that includes those audio/video issues in the published version. If we can't live with anything less than "NPR quality," live video is probably not our best option.

*More Guest Issues:* Live video isn't universal yet, so guests don't always show up on time and prepared for live video. Do live video for any length of time and you'll see every possible scenario—guests with no webcam, terrible hotel WiFi, or even calling in from a moving vehicle.

Since we can't control other people, the best we can do is have a backup plan. Keep a list of topics and questions we can answer on the fly, and be mentally prepared to go live without the guest on any given episode.

My personal favorite scenario for live video shows is to have a reliable co-host. That way, even if a guest cancels last-minute or joins late, the show continues.

**Live Video Checklist**

Live video might be right for us if we are…

- quick on our feet and calm under pressure
- able to come up with 15 minutes of content on the fly
- disciplined and consistent in following our own schedule
- willing to invest extra time in guest prep and promotion
- willing to push through any initial discomfort
- willing to learn and work through tech issues
- more concerned with real-time feedback and energy than perfection
- already active on social platforms that favor live video

Now that we've looked at the benefits and drawbacks of live video, let's look at how podcasts are traditionally recorded. We'll also look at why I chose not to broadcast the *MicroFamous* podcast on live video.

Recording behind the scenes, without a live audience, removes a lot of variables. As a result, it's less demanding and gives us a higher level of control over the final product.

Guests who show up late or cancel last-minute can simply be rescheduled. We don't have to fill time or come up with content on the spot. We don't have to pay attention to a live audience or keep an eye on live comments and questions, either.

We have much more flexibility and control with editing. When audio/video issues come up, we can simply pause, address the issues, and pick up the conversation. The same applies to content issues or concerns, such as when a guest says something they regret, or gives the wrong URL. Those sections can simply be re-recorded or removed in editing.

**Pre-Recorded Video Checklist**

Recording behind the scenes might be a better fit if we...

- want absolute control over the final product
- want to record custom introductions for each episode
- want to record episodes in batches, rather than a regular "live" time slot
- want to record episodes in advance and release them over time
- want to accommodate bigger guests with hectic schedules
- need flexibility in our own schedule due to frequent travel or speaking gigs
- don't want to go live without a guest
- are in an older industry where live video will limit our ability to book quality guests

If the answer to a majority of those is Yes (as it was for me with the MicroFamous podcast), recording behind the scenes is probably our best option. We can always switch to live video later, or mix live episodes into our show for a fun change of pace.

Given that live video is still in the early stages, here is our recommendation for any thought leader looking at launching a podcast.

Start simple, build good hosting skills, then add more variables.

Start by recording video behind the scenes, and get comfortable having great conversations with influencers and thought leaders. Then start experimenting with live video *alone*, having one-way conversations with the Audience.

Then experiment by inviting other influencers onto live episodes, starting with friends or colleagues. This ensures that issues that arise with live video won't put new relationships at risk.

By approaching live video in simple steps and adding variables gradually, we build a good foundation and a comfort level with live video. When tech issues arise or a guest shows up late, we can fall back on our ability to have one-way conversations and deal with any issues on the spot.

Choosing between live video and pre-recorded is a personal and strategic decision. The good news is there is no bad option. The goal is to find the balance between a style that plays to our strengths while being in the places our Audience is paying attention.

# 10X ROI: Running a Profitable Podcast

In the world of MicroFamous, a podcast is profitable and sustainable when it delivers a 10x return on our investment. How do we build this kind of podcast?

Here are four key elements.

We don't necessarily need all these elements when we first launch our podcast, but our goal should be to put all four in place as fast as possible.

### Clear & Compelling Idea

Our podcast title, tagline, and description must work together to deliver our Clear & Compelling Idea that leads to our unique Point of View.

It's critical to avoid common mistakes we see in new podcasts, such as being more *clever* than clear, or choosing podcast artwork for our personal style rather than a style that appeals to our ideal clients. Remember, the podcast isn't just about us; it's about the people we want to teach, train and lead.

### Vision

We must build a clear vision by mapping out the number of clients, speaking gigs, book sales, or program sales required to hit a 10x return on the time and energy we're investing into our podcast.

If we know exactly who we want to serve and impact, we can clarify our vision and set good expectations for our podcast.

I think the biggest opportunities in podcasting right now are in small, lucrative niches. Despite starting a popular podcast with a mainstream audience in my first niche, my biggest wins in podcasting haven't come from the podcast with 1 million+ downloads.

My biggest wins have come from helping thought leaders become MicroFamous in very focused niches.

By starting with a focused podcast aimed at the Few instead of the Many, we can produce a 10x ROI faster because our content generates demand for high-ticket offers like coaching and consulting.

This happens to our clients consistently. A potential client stumbles across them online, binges on their podcast, comes out with new beliefs, reaches out and gets on a sales call with the intention to sign up as a client.

There's a predictable, straight line: podcast ⟶ high-ticket sales. The closer we get to that clear, straight line, the more we have a clear vision of 10x ROI from our podcast.

What if we don't have a high-ticket offer, or what if our content is better suited for a mainstream audience? It's a different challenge, so we need a different vision.

To reach a mainstream audience, we must have an idea so Clear and Compelling to a large group of people that it has the potential to spread by earned media. That means podcast interviews, blog features, industry articles, and traditional PR.

If we have that Clear & Compelling Idea and our goal is to serve a mainstream audience, our vision needs to be built around small-ticket metrics like book sales, program and course sales, and membership site sales.

## Tracking

The simplest form of tracking is to make our podcast our main platform, the centerpiece of our New Media Machine.

If our podcast is just another channel for content that's already available in other places, our podcast won't have a great chance to attract an audience and build momentum.

If we have several platforms, all competing for attention, and don't have great tracking in place, we won't be able to track ROI back to the podcast even when it *is* working.

Outside of all the technical options for lead tracking, the simplest form of lead tracking starts with our sales calls. By asking prospects how they came to be on that sales call, and tracking the answers, we can tell if our podcast is impacting prospects' decision-making process.

By putting great tracking in place, or making our podcast the centerpiece of our New Media Machine, we ensure that we're tracking ROI back to the podcast versus our other methods.

## Relationship-Building System

We must capitalize on the relationship opportunities created by running a podcast. Every time we have a guest on our podcast and they don't hear from us for the next year, we just missed a massive opportunity.

By putting all of our podcast guests into a Relationship-Building System, we ensure that we turn those potential relationships into a powerful network of strategic partners, champions and advocates.

A network like this can generate high-quality, high-trust referrals for years or decades. We can't let that opportunity slip by and expect a 10x ROI from our podcast.

So, our ideal is to have a podcast that...

- serves as our primary new media platform
- delivers a Clear & Compelling Idea
- leading to a unique Point of View
- that attracts the right people
- in way that generates demand for our services
- producing sales and trackable ROI
- while creating opportunities for life-changing relationships with influencers and thought leaders.

When we don't have these elements in place, the consequences may not show up for 6 to 12 months, yet they always show up. So, the faster we can build those four elements, the better our chances are to build a podcast that generates 10x ROI.

# Lead Gen Podcast—The Pros and Cons

Once thought leaders and influencers realized we could simply invite our ideal clients on to our podcast as guests, we created something new; *the lead generation podcast*, a podcast that can be used to generate conversations with people we want to buy our service.

This is very different from using a podcast to teach, train, and lead our Audience.

In a lead generation podcast, the conversations are essentially the "Get to Know You" part of a sales call. They include virtually the same questions we would ask in a discovery call or sales consultation.

By definition, potential clients are people who still suffer from the problem we solve. *That means they won't have success in that area to share.* They probably won't share many of our key beliefs either. So we have to be strategic on how we frame the conversation.

Our focus of the conversation isn't just to give the guest a platform to look good and share interesting content. The focus of the conversation is to drive home their need for a solution to their problem.

To do this, we focus on their journey and how they have overcome the smaller problems that lead up to the problem we solve. This often leads to their beliefs and values, their current stage, and their strategy for moving forward.

If they are truly an ideal client, there should be more thought-provoking silences in those conversations than we would normally hear on a podcast. Why? Because we should be asking thought-provoking questions. Questions that agitate the problem and their frustration.

We should be asking questions that uncover differences in beliefs, weak areas in their business, or strategic plans that don't line up with their goals.

All these things should lead them to want to have a conversation with us behind the scenes, because our Clear & Compelling Idea perfectly hits their current problem.

If we're not having conversations behind the scenes that turn into sales, there are two possibilities. Either we're not inviting the right people as guests, or we're not delivering a Clear & Compelling Idea during the podcast that makes them want to continue the conversation behind the scenes.

When running a lead gen podcast, the audience is secondary. The focus is on the guest, which means audience growth needs to take a backseat. The conversations we have with guests on a lead gen podcast often aren't as fun and free-flowing as conversations with thought leaders. So, if we decide to take this approach, lean into it and don't worry about the audience growth.

What if we need sales opportunities now, yet we understand the value of running a podcast that serves as our leadership platform?

No problem. We aren't locked into one approach. We can start as a lead gen podcast,fill our sales pipeline with guests, and later transition to focus on leading our Audience.

That's why Freedom of Movement is such an important part of the MicroFamous strategy. When we build the right strategy and brand for our podcast from the beginning, it makes this kind of shift easier. In fact, by creating the right podcast title, we can simply change the tagline later when we shift focus.

It's also possible to hit a middle ground—a podcast that reaches a small, lucrative niche, featuring a mix of potential clients, fellow thought leaders and strategic referral partners.

That approach allows us to build strategic long-term referral relationships with thought leaders while also featuring prospects as guests. It makes for a more interesting show for our Audience while still building up a short-term sales pipeline.

Whichever approach we use for our podcast, the real key is to focus on our goals while keeping our expectations in line with our MicroFamous strategy.

CREATE QUICK WINS

# Create Quick Wins

Just because the biggest results from podcasting accumulate over time doesn't mean we can't have Quick Wins along the way.

In the early months of our podcast, there is one key tactic we recommend to deliver Quick Wins. Turn the new relationships with guests into strategic referral partnerships, collaborative marketing, joint venture projects, and similar short-term promotion opportunities.

By looking at our podcast as a pipeline for new, valuable relationships, we can get tangible results from our podcast regardless of the size of our audience.

While other types of new media are important, over the long run, our podcast will deliver our best results. Our podcast is our platform to teach, train and lead our Audience. It's where we cultivate new beliefs, the key to creating ideal clients.

Let's say we feature two influencers on our podcast each month.

When we build and accelerate those relationships, here are the results.

We have...

- interviewed 24 people we probably wouldn't have met otherwise
- built rapport and brought value to 24 influential people
- added those 24 influencers to our network and stayed in touch via email, social media, and personal follow-ups
- connected those 24 people to each other through our podcast and by direct introduction
- looked for opportunities to send them business and build goodwill
- connected with those 24 influencers at events or conferences

- created 24 different ways to bring value to our clients by introducing them to influencers who are each experts in their field
- created a network of 24 influencers in the world looking for ways to send us ideal clients because we're doing the same for them

While our podcast builds momentum and starts to attract an Audience of the right people, we leverage the relationships with influencers behind the scenes to generate referrals, joint ventures, and speaking opportunities.

In other words, we use our podcast to build a powerful strategic referral network in just 12 months. That's how we generate Quick Wins in the first year of our podcast.

# HOW PODCASTS

# GROW

# How Podcasts Grow

Most of the advice on growing a podcast is based on a widely held belief: podcasts grow due to flurries of activity and clever growth hacks.

On the contrary, I believe that most of the battles for podcast growth are won or lost before a show ever launches. When we launch a podcast that is part of a MicroFamous strategy, we give ourselves the best chance to build a successful podcast that grows organically.

When podcasts are launched without a MicroFamous strategy, we can try all the hacks and growth tactics in the world, and we can goose the numbers here and there, but the fundamentals don't change.

Which is why most of the questions on podcast growth I hear are really just different forms of the same question...

"How can I get X company to CHOOSE me and put my podcast in front of lots of people for free?"

Now, I would never discourage thought leaders from thinking of creative ways to put their podcast in front of more people.

*Yet if a show isn't growing organically, I don't believe most growth hacks will work.*

While I've seen temporary boosts in audience numbers, they are rarely permanent, which makes sense. Easy come, easy go.

I've spent time with thought leaders who get free traffic from social platforms or viral videos, so they receive an influx of new people into their audience.

They often find these new people incredibly hard to monetize.

They are wildly unqualified, they don't have the beliefs needed to buy, they take far more nurturing than expected before buying and, in the end, they might simply be the wrong people.

That's not counting the *opportunity cost.*

Every minute we spend trying to get a platform to choose us and put our podcast in front of people for free is time we're not spending on tactics that build our Audience methodically.

It's time we're NOT spending on proven tactics with a higher chance of success, such as getting featured on other podcasts, engaging with our Audience on social media, or maximizing our existing email list.

Years ago, one of our clients launched a group coaching program that brought in $40k in sales from an email list of 500 people. There is massive opportunity in small groups of the *right* people.

There will always be new, interesting opportunities for free traffic, and *free traffic is never truly free.* Chasing these opportunities is an investment of time, resources, and mental energy.

Yet for a podcast that...

- delivers a Clear & Compelling Idea
- to the right Audience
- which is growing through word of mouth
- building momentum and leadership in a lucrative niche

there's nothing wrong with experimenting a bit with free traffic sources.

However, our new media efforts should never be dependent on platforms giving us free traffic. Remember, easy come, easy go.

The best approach for our podcast is to attract an Audience, build influence, and become famously influential to the right people - systematically.

# How to Build Win-Win Sponsorships

At the heart of any successful sponsorship is a Win-Win scenario for the podcast host and the sponsor.

Many thought leaders have an eye on sponsorship dollars, especially to offset production costs. As more money flows into podcasting, this creates an opportunity for those who can build win-win sponsorships.

However, before we get to specific recommendations, it's important to understand this principle:

*To create a true Win-Win for a podcast sponsor, we must be able to inspire our Audience to take action.* So, any discussion of sponsorship should start by looking at Calls to Action.

**Calls to Action are a form of withdrawal.** We draw on the bank of trust and authority we've built with a group people to get them to take an action we recommend.

**Calls to Action are limited.** We have a limited number of "withdrawals" before breaking trust and losing our authority with our Audience.

For example, too many direct calls to action in an email list will cause people to tune out and stop opening our emails. There's even a well-known term for this: "burning the list." The more calls to action we stuff into a podcast episode, the more we risk burning our Audience in the same way.

**Calls to Action are precious.** Each opportunity we have to make a withdrawal against the trust and authority we've built is valuable and should be treated with respect and consideration.

Once we agree that Calls to Action are limited, precious forms of withdrawal, it puts us in the right frame to talk about sponsorships.

Here's the real question for sponsorships: *Is this limited, precious form of withdrawal worth giving to someone else's product or service?*

In some cases, the answer may be Yes.

Yet for thought leaders, especially those with a high-ticket offer, the answer is usually No. So, why are sponsorships such a big question in thought leader circles? *Because sponsorship money feels like extra money.* It goes into a different mental bucket.

Let's say we land a big sponsorship deal with a company in our space. We get $5,000 a month and it goes into the sponsorship bucket.

To get that money, we have to promote the sponsor in every podcast episode, plus via email and social media.

Doesn't sound like a lot, but those are all forms of withdrawal on our trust and authority *that do nothing to draw people closer to us.* They do nothing to draw people into our high-ticket offer where we can make a real difference in their business.

If we have a $5,000 offer, sending those calls to action somewhere else, even if it costs us just *one* sale a month, completely wipes out the benefit of the sponsorship.

Yet we don't see it that way because the sponsorship money lives in its own mental bucket, and we never see the lost money from sales we *would* have made.

That's what we have to lose—tangible sales of our high-ticket offer—obscured by the sponsorship money that goes into a different mental bucket. So, sponsorships aren't an automatic win for us as a podcast host.

Then we have to look at the other side of the relationship—the sponsor. Without a mutually beneficial relationship, we'll burn through sponsors on a regular basis.

Here are the conditions for sponsorships to work for the sponsors.

**Sponsors must be the right match for our Audience.**

Without a good match, we won't have the freedom to authentically, enthusiastically recommend their offer. People can smell a paid endorsement a mile away.

This also means there can't be a huge mismatch in the style or personality of the sponsor compared to our audience. Sending our audience to a sponsor that treats them differently or speaks a different "language" will hurt the trust and authority we've built.

**Sponsors must solve a related problem.**

Without this close link between the sponsor and the problems our clients experience, we end up diluting our Clear & Compelling Idea, making our entire podcast less effective.

The sponsor's offer should solve a problem that comes before or after the problem we solve. If I had to choose between the two, I'd choose sponsors that help people solve the problem that comes *before* the problem I solve. That way, when the Audience takes the sponsor's offer and gets results, they are now positioned to need my offer even more.

**Sponsors must solve that problem effectively—delivering real results to their clients.**

Without the element of real results, we risk breaking the trust and losing the authority we've built with our Audience. Every Call to Action puts our reputation on the line. Each member of our Audience that takes a sponsor's offer and doesn't see results is a ticking time bomb of negativity. The only question is, how vocal and connected are they?

**Sponsors must see real ROI.**

Without trackable leads that produce sales, the sponsorship relationship will never be stable and reliable. So, not only does our Audience need to be a good match, we must have the trust and authority with our Audience to drive real action.

This is why sponsorships are often tough to justify over the long run.

If we have the trust and authority to drive real action from our Audience, why would we make withdrawals on that trust and authority to promote some other offer?

**Here are specific cases where sponsorships can work effectively long-term.**

*We don't offer a high-profit, high-impact service.*

A good example would be thought leaders who primarily speak and write books, or sell low-cost programs and online courses to a large mainstream audience. We need to build relationships with large numbers of people to generate real revenue and often need to monetize that audience in multiple ways to maximize our profit.

In this case, sponsorships can generate more revenue from a large audience by offering products and services that are complementary. Ideally, these products and services help people solve a related problem and are consistent with our Clear & Compelling Idea, so we don't undercut demand for our products.

*We offer a high-profit, high-impact offer—but only in very small windows of heavy promotion.*

Thought leaders who make one or two big yearly pushes for a signature program fall into this category. We have specific times of heavy promotion, and long periods of time in between where we can promote other offers.

*We have a long-term commitment from the sponsor.*

Good long-term decisions aren't based on revenue from temporary or open-ended sponsorship agreements. Long-term commitments and clear expectations are the foundation of good long-term sponsorship decisions.

Ideally, a long-term commitment is reached only after a pilot project with good tracking, so the sponsorship is based on a realistic percentage of the ROI the sponsor expects.

As you can see, these are very specific cases and involve more work than most sponsors and thought leaders are willing to invest.

Yet without these elements, how can we have a successful, mutually beneficial relationship that delivers real ROI to both sides?

That's why I strongly encourage every thought leader with a high-ticket offer to invest Calls to Action—those limited, precious forms of withdrawal—on our own offers.

# Podcast Stats in the World of MicroFamous

Podcast stats are a two-edged sword. While being a good metric for growth, stats certainly aren't the only measure of success.

Podcast stats can also be a bottomless rabbit hole many podcast hosts fall down, obsessing over stats to the detriment of the business behind the podcast.

One well-known podcaster made the comment that she likes a particular stats tracker that tells her where she ranks on podcast charts by country. Her reason being, "The goal is to beat the competition."

Yet that begs the question, beat them in what? **Being first on a podcast chart doesn't mean we're first in the minds of our ideal clients.**

Does Gucci define success by comparing their sales numbers to Old Navy?

Does Rolex define success by comparing sales numbers to Timex?

Does BMW define success by comparing sales numbers to Toyota?

In other words, podcast charts alone can't tell us if we are famously influential to the *right* people.

In fact, once we understand the Many and the Few, and our goal is to become MicroFamous, stats become a less reliable metric of success. Going after download numbers and chart rankings leads us down the path of appealing to the Many, not the Few.

**And the Few is where the profit and impact lives.**

When I look at our podcast production clients, no one is getting stalked by paparazzi outside an LA nightclub. Yet they all have multi-6 and 7-figure businesses.

Why? Because they're MicroFamous.

And we can all be MicroFamous. We just need to find the right people and focus all our efforts on becoming famously influential to them.

So, what is the function of podcast stats?

There are three key metrics I encourage clients to keep an eye on.

- Downloads in the last 30 days
- Most popular episode of all time
- Download numbers for that episode

In just three metrics, we can get a sense of whether we're building momentum or not. Here's how we look at each of these metrics.

**Key Podcast Metrics**

*Downloads in the last 30 days*—If monthly download numbers aren't growing consistently, or growth comes from unusual spikes we can't explain, we may have a problem in the branding or positioning of the podcast.

*Most popular episode of all time*—If this episode isn't being replaced on a regular basis, the growth in our subscriber base has stalled. As our subscriber base grows, newer episodes should dethrone older episodes as Most Popular Episode of All Time.

*Download number of our most popular episode*—This gives us the upper range of our downloads per episode. The average episode gets around 200 downloads. Established niche business podcasts are probably in the 500-5,000 range of downloads per episode.

So, if the metrics are going up, and the most popular episode is being replaced on a regular basis, it tells us we have a healthy show with a growing Audience.

Of course, there are other stats that can be helpful, and newer stats will come along that shed light on things we can improve. Apple Podcasts gives us the ability to see the percentage of an episode our Audience consumes, which can tell us if our average episode is too long or we have the wrong episode format. (Apple also records subscriber numbers, but they are not made public.)

Yet we always want to keep this in mind: **The only metrics that matter are the metrics we use to make better decisions.**

That's why we boil down any metrics tracking to the top three. Anything more than that gets overwhelming and becomes white noise.

Now let's look at other indicators that we are reaching our goal of becoming MicroFamous.

**Other podcast success indicators**

*Replies to promo emails and social media posts*—Current research shows no hard correlation between social media engagement and sales, especially easy engagement such as likes and shares. But comments and email replies take real effort. They can be an indication that our podcast is resonating and attracting attention in our niche.

*Mentions at industry events*—Niche thought leaders, especially our clients, often get a ton of positive feedback on their podcast when they show up at conferences, trade shows, and speaking gigs.

*Prospective clients referencing the podcast on sales calls*—This indicates that the podcast is doing its job of converting beliefs, building trust and authority, and creating demand for our service.

*Fellow thought leaders mentioning our podcast publicly*—This can indicate that we're building a good following among the Few in our niche. Social proof from fellow thought leaders will become more and more important as people become less trusting overall.

*Inclusion in curated lists*—When trade publications or brands put our podcast on "Best Of" and "Top 10" lists, it adds another layer of credibility and authority, even for publications that aren't well-trafficked online. It's another credibility indicator for our "Featured In" section of our website, landing pages, sales pages, follow-up emails, and much more.

Yet with all those indicators of success, it's tempting to get drawn into chasing chart rankings, growth hacking, and efforts to game the system. After all, it's the main topic of conversation between podcast hosts.

It all comes down to one goal, which I believe, in most cases, is a fantasy.

We are looking for the mother of all shortcuts: a big company to give us thousands of new followers for free. That's where all the growth hacking, gaming the system, and trying to climb the iTunes charts comes from.

It's the same fantasy that fueled the success of American Idol. We're like a musician who can't pay the bills, looking for a record company to rescue us from the work of building our Audience one fan, one show, one album at a time. But in the end, relentless, methodical, systematic growth is the best kind of growth.

Celebrity can be built overnight. Real influence can't.

# How to Choose Our Social Platform

For many thought leaders, social media is one of the key sources of complexity and stress in our business.

If we simply go along with the herd, we find ourselves on a bunch of different social platforms, creating a bunch of "rogue" content, trying to be everywhere for everyone.

So either we end up glued to our phone, or feeling guilty for not being glued to our phone. That's the daily reality for most thought leaders, and it sounds like a terrible way to live.

When we have a New Media Machine, our social media strategy is very different. Our goal isn't to be everywhere; our goal is to be famously influential to the right people.

So our social media strategy is...

- build ONE great social platform
- creating connection, conversation and community
- while leading our Audience back to our podcast
- where we can lead them to new beliefs and new actions
- so we help them take new action
- and get new results

If our social media strategy is based on building ONE great social platform, how do we choose the right platform? How do we show up in the right place for the right people?

For thought leaders, the best social platform is the one where our ideal clients are already active and they're asking us to show up there.

The next-best social platform is a place where our ideal clients are hanging out and there is no dominant thought leader.

This is especially true if our ideal clients are looking for content on how to solve their problems. By creating that content, we fill a genuine need, and we pull the right people to us, rather than trying to push content at them.

On the other end of the spectrum, the worst reason to jump on a social platform is that it worked for someone else. Why? Because there will never be a social platform without a success story. We simply won't hear about the failures.

On top of that, the explosive growth of a social platform itself creates its own success stories. In other words, an influencer catches a social platform at the right time, and the platform puts them in front of lots of new people as the platform grows. It's a lottery event. Nothing wrong with that, yet we can't make good decisions on the expectation that we will hit the social media "lottery."

It also helps to take success stories with a healthy dose of skepticism. After all, even the success stories aren't always as successful as we think. Behind the scenes, we often find thought leaders struggling to monetize their audience. Which really means they're struggling to solve a big, valuable problem and tell people about it in a clear and compelling way.

As thought leaders, the best time to jump on a social platform is on the cusp of an explosive growth phase, after the early adopters have worked out some of the kinks, yet before our competition jumps on the bandwagon. If we aren't in that time frame, it's best to plan on slower growth and commit to growing our Audience methodically.

What's the ideal social platform for our New Media Machine? Where can we show up, attract attention, and lead people back to our podcast?

We're looking for a platform where our social micro-content can start real conversations and build a sense of connection and community.

To do this, we need a clear and compelling reason to be on that social platform, and our micro-content must be created or customized just for that platform.

Our challenge is to give our Audience a clear and compelling reason to follow us on that platform. If we don't make it crystal clear, our social platform will struggle to grow by word of mouth, which is the foundation of real growth.

**Social Platform Checklist**

Here is a simple checklist of questions to help us choose the right social platform:

Do we have a Clear & Compelling Idea to share?

Are our ideal clients hanging out on that platform?

Are they using that platform to find content on how to solve their problem?

Are they asking us to show up there?

Can we have a natural conversation on that platform?

Does this social platform have explosive growth potential, or is it already mature and saturated with competitors?

Have early adopters worked out the kinks, or will we have to work out the kinks?

If we knew it wasn't any easier to build an audience on a new platform, would we switch?

Questions like these help expose our true motivation and reveal the key information we need to make a good decision.

The toughest part about attracting an audience on social platforms is commitment. Learning a new social platform takes time, just like any new skillset. The skills we've built on other platforms don't automatically carry over.

It takes take some time and experimentation to find the right type of content for each social platform, the content that resonates with our Audience, creating conversation, connection, and community.

Dabbling in a bunch of different platforms simply won't get us through that experimentation phase to the point of truly becoming MicroFamous.

A good indication of our level of commitment is how quickly we commit. If we're actually serious about succeeding on a new social platform, we won't jump too quickly. We won't dabble. We will do our homework and commit to experiment till we find the content that actually brings in clients, not just attention.

The MicroFamous strategy calls for clear thinking in choosing our social platform followed by 100% commitment to that platform.

# Build, Share, & Engage Around Micro-Content

Once we commit to building one great social platform, we can't just post our micro-content and run. That's one of the biggest mistakes we make as thought leaders: we want to attract attention and followers on a social platform without the hard work of engaging with them.

Without real engagement, our social platform won't produce real clients, real sales, and real impact. So, any plans for social media must include time for us to engage with our Audience around our micro-content.

Our New Media Machine helps turn long-form content (like podcast episodes) into micro-content, allowing us to speed up content creation so we can focus more on conversation, connection, and community.

Our goal for micro-content is to find what works for us, reverse-engineer it, and turn it into a system. Invest some extra time today to make tomorrow easier.

First, we create micro-content, inspired by podcast episodes, that starts real conversations with our Audience. If it doesn't start conversations, scrap it and experiment till we find something that does.

These could be highlight clips, audiograms, excerpts, text posts, graphics, quotes, and much more. The forms of micro-content will evolve and change with every platform. Fortunately, there will never be a shortage of people experimenting with new tactics. Follow the best, steal the tactics that work, and throw out everything else.

Once we've created micro-content that starts conversations, we engage around that micro-content to keep the conversations going. The more conversations we have, the more we draw people into a deeper level of connection and relationship.

*Then we aim to move the conversation off the social platform*, first by promoting our podcast and steering attention there. If we handle our own sales process, we can also take those conversations into message apps, email, or phone calls. (This is the missing step in turning social media into sales—proactively creating real offline conversations.)

Once we find what works, we can build a system to speed up the content creation and publishing. The highest-leverage solution is to pull micro-content directly from our podcast interviews and episodes of our own podcast.

We build a simple micro-content system in three steps.

First, we *automate* through tech, tools, and software.

With AI and machine learning, everything is getting easier, including turning podcasts and videos into accurate transcriptions, converting text into videos, or turning blog posts into slick-looking ebooks. The tools have never been better, faster, or cheaper.

As this trend continues, it will empower our Assistant to create more micro-content in less time.

High-level design, audio/video editing, or desktop publishing skills may become unnecessary because tech, tools, and software will handle most of the heavy lifting. This also means that the ideas and beliefs conveyed in our micro-content will be far more important than the tech skills required to produce it.

Second, we *delegate* through systems and people.

There is always a way to systematize content creation. *Nothing is so high level that we are the only ones who can do it.* With a little imagination and experimentation, virtually any form of micro-content can be created consistently as part of our New Media Machine.

Third, we *provide resources*—the materials, tools, training, checklists, and software our Assistant needs to produce micro-content.

A great example from the design world is a style guide. This resource helps non-designers understand how to use keep a brand consistent across many different materials and uses.

We can do the same for our Assistant by providing resources, tools, and software they can use, along with checklists and guides they can follow to produce the exact micro-content we want.

Using simple systems, all elements of our New Media Machine work together, allowing us to invest our time and focus into engaging around our content, rather than simply creating more content.

The more time we spend engaging, creating conversations, connection, and community, the more effective our social platform becomes.

# How to Leverage a New Media Machine at Every Stage

The new media landscape is shifting to reward clear and compelling ideas backed by real engagement.

Of course, this makes sense because it matches the way real groups of people behave in tribes with an influential leader.

Political leaders understand this. They build their voting base on the campaign trail through a combination of stump speeches and personal interaction (kissing babies).

Religious leaders also understand this. They build their congregation through a combination of regular sermons and personal interaction with members before and after church services.

*Clear and compelling ideas backed by real engagement.*

We can do the same in our business, and our New Media Machine makes it systematic, consistent, and streamlined.

By handling all the new media activities that don't require personal involvement, our New Media Machine gives us leverage and consistency, while freeing up our time, energy, and focus.

As thought leaders, our business goes through different stages, each with different challenges. Let's look at how our New Media Machine works at each stage, positioning us to move forward into the next stage.

**Figure-it-Out Stage**

This is where we're working solo and throwing mud against the wall to see what sticks. It often involves a lot of individual client work and we're doing a bunch of different things for those clients.

In this stage, we're playing with service packages, learning who we enjoy serving, and building expertise by solving real problems for real clients.

Our biggest challenges are:

- being easily found and visible to potential clients
- becoming known for solving real problems for real people
- attracting ideal clients consistently
- increasing our fees

We need a way to bring in new clients without investing a ton of time, because we're still doing some (or all) of the client work ourselves.

Often at this stage, time-heavy methods like speaking gigs, networking events, conferences, and other forms of personal marketing are most effective for us. We probably aren't super profitable yet, so cash-heavy tactics like paid ads and sales funnels are probably out of the question.

Our New Media Machine helps us meet those challenges by publishing content that works 24/7 to attract an Audience and build influence. When we're winning the Battle for Attention without being glued to our phone, we can provide great service, improve our systems, and deliver great results for our clients.

## Growing Pains Stage

In the next stage, we're feeling the progress, but it's also painful. We have enough clients to keep us busy, but we're still doing most of the work ourselves. We're working way too much, staying up too late, feeling out of control, and worrying if the business will "work."

It's often the fork in the road, where we've built real expertise, but now we have to make major decisions on how we're going to monetize our expertise. Big decisions that will determine the future of our business.

Our biggest challenges are

- delivering great service to current clients
- streamlining our service offering
- attracting more ideal clients
- selling higher-profit services

On top of all that, we start to face big decisions on how to position ourselves in the world, how to structure our business, and where to put our focus.

As we gain more experience in our business, we start to question what kind of business we truly want and how to get there. These kind of decisions take mental and emotional space.

It's at this stage when it's most tempting to slack off on building authority or being visible. Our New Media Machine is the key to preventing the feast-or-famine cycle.

While most thought leaders get stuck in this cycle, we move forward. We can be methodical and relentless, knowing that our New Media Machine is working 24/7 to keep us visible, build authority, create relationships, and attract ideal clients.

Once we make the big decisions, we can package our offer, streamline our services, sharpen our focus, and move forward into the next stage.

**Scaling Stage**

We know exactly who we want to serve, what we sell, and how to sell more. We have our service dialed in, and we know how to deliver that service to a much bigger group of people at a profit.

Best of all, we've either captured a leadership position in a lucrative niche or we're breathing down the neck of the leader.

We're ready to make a Big Move.

Our biggest challenges are

- refining our systems
- bringing in the right people
- delivering great service that generates referrals and word-of-mouth
- shortening sales cycles and destroying objections in advance
- closing a consistent, predictable stream of ideal clients
- being more visible and building unstoppable momentum in our niche

Most importantly, our challenge is to do all of this with less of our personal time, effort, and energy.

At this point, our New Media Machine forms the foundation we can build on to explode our influence and scale up.

We can pour ourselves into people and systems, especially in operations and sales, while our New Media Machine works 24/7 to keep us visible online, drive home our Clear & Compelling Idea, and draw the right people into our Audience where we can keep in touch.

As the centerpiece of our New Media Machine, our podcast serves a critical role as an incubator, cultivating the right beliefs and creating demand for our service, which is now dialed in and scalable.

Through our podcast we shine a spotlight on our happy clients and turn their experiences into Success Story episodes. This helps our Audience see a vision of themselves solving their problem while instilling the trust that our offer is the right solution for them.

All this frees up mental and emotional energy. We can focus on sharing our Clear & Compelling Idea everywhere, creating real engagement, and becoming famously influential to the right people. We are free to be creative in how we talk to people, in how we reach new people, and in how we strengthen relationships with the people we influence.

At the scaling stage, our New Media Machine allows us to have fun in our business, becoming known for ONE thing, and getting paid more for being MicroFamous than for providing a service.

From starting to scaling, each stage of a thought leader business has unique challenges. By making our efforts systematic, consistent, and streamlined, our New Media Machine frees up the time, energy, and focus we need to overcome challenges at each stage and become MicroFamous.

# Hiring a New Media Assistant

One of the biggest mistakes thought leaders make is fighting the Battle for Attention alone.

We typically handle all of our own new media, using our "spare time" to be active on social media, pitch ourselves to podcasts, and perform the daily essentials of becoming MicroFamous.

Or we assign our new media efforts to someone on our team who already has a thousand other responsibilities.

Unfortunately, in both cases, it rarely works out.

The reason is human nature. People can't have two top priorities. Something must come first, and everything else gets put on the back burner.

For those who serve clients individually or in small groups, client work virtually always takes that top priority. Which means our new media efforts are inconsistent, sporadic, and lower quality than our client work. Why would we expect those types of efforts to be successful or effective?

That's why we recommend hiring a New Media Assistant; it's one of the critical first steps in building a New Media Machine.

Our Assistant runs the daily essentials, pitching us on podcasts, scheduling interviews and creating micro-content, all at a high level of quality and consistency.

Once our Assistant is up to speed, we also get the control and customization we need to get better results over time.

Fortunately, it's never been easier to find and hire great New Media Assistants. We start by making a few key decisions.

Overseas vs Home Country

In-person vs Remote

Part-Time vs Full-Time

For thought leaders hiring their first New Media Assistant, we recommend a basic set of criteria:

An overseas, part-time, remote freelancer working from home with no requirement for phone contact with clients.

We can look for this person by posting ads on sites like Indeed and Upwork, using freelancer marketplaces like FreeeUp, or going straight to overseas job boards like OnlineJobs.ph.

In the job ad, we recommend asking for a cover letter sharing why they are a good fit for the job, along with examples of their work for other clients.

When reviewing candidates, we recommend looking for indications of these ideal traits and behaviors:

- steady and patient
- likes having rules and systems
- prefers repetitive work, clear standards, and predictable outputs
- good communication
- punctual and prepared
- clear and concise writing

We recommend immediately screening out anyone who doesn't supply a well-written cover letter that shows a mastery of the English language.

Once we have a crop of candidates, we can put them through a simple initial screening to identify the top candidates. This initial screening can be questionnaire, a 15-minute Skype call, or a recorded video interview through a tool like Spark Hire.

Once they pass an initial screening, we put them through a skills assessment that's as realistic as possible based on the actual work. We also request they complete a personality/behavior assessment like the DISC or Meyers-Briggs.

The skills and behavior assessment stage will eliminate most candidates, and probably leave one or two final candidates.

The final test is a short-term project with a defined, measurable output.

We can either send the top candidate through this project, or, if it makes financial sense, we can put two or three final candidates through this project. An example project might be to successfully secure two podcast interviews for us, using their own research and a basic pitch email template.

Once they have successfully completed that project, we select the best candidate and make them an offer. The goal is to contract with them to produce a specific set of services each month in exchange for a flat fee, paid to them in advance at the beginning of the month.

This forces us to set clear expectations with clear metrics and gives our Assistant a clear incentive to work effectively and efficiently.

Once we have our Assistant on board, pitching us on podcasts is the best place for them to start. Securing podcast interviews that help us reach niche audiences, grow our email list, and build our influence is one of the most valuable tasks an Assistant can do for us.

One good podcast interview a month might bring enough referrals and sales to offset months of their fees. Then we can add more responsibilities and raise their monthly fee as we add more systems to our New Media Machine.

When we steadily ramp them up and make expectations clear, we avoid pitfalls, keep quality and efficiency high, and build systems for future Assistants along the way.

Every thought leader needs allies in the Battle for Attention, and our first ally is a New Media Assistant.

# Running the Machine

A New Media Machine isn't complicated. It is beautifully simple, operating on three key steps repeated on a regular basis. These steps are the fundamentals—the "blocking and tackling" of our New Media Machine.

They are planning, reporting, and regular meetings.

Planning on the front end

Reporting on the back end

Regular meetings in between

We recommend monthly planning meetings to set strategic objectives, looking 60 to 90 days ahead to leverage upcoming interviews, podcast episodes, events, and other opportunities.

During those monthly planning meetings we set clear expectations for our Assistant. This helps keep everyone on the same page about the performance we expect, and closes out projects and assignments with backend reporting.

Then we simply use weekly meetings to keep things on track.

We may be tempted to set goals for our Assistant based on the results we want: engagement, downloads, shares, and so on. Those are outcome goals, and our Assistant doesn't have the control to be held accountable to that type of goals.

It's our role as the leader to translate the outcomes we want into performance goals for our Assistant. What are they expected to *do* that will produce the outcomes we want?

A good set of performance goals for an Assistant is publishing one episode of our podcast, getting us featured on one podcast, and posting micro-content two or three times per day on social media. Assuming we give them the raw content, those are performance goals an Assistant has control over. Those are the goals to which we can hold them accountable.

That means we also need to set performance goals for ourselves. What are we going to do to produce the outcomes we want? How many interviews are we committing to? How many podcast episodes are we recording and when? How much time are we setting aside to engage with our Audience? Accountability is best when it's a two-way street. By committing to our performance goals, and following through, we inspire our Assistant to do the same.

Whenever we slack off on one of the fundamentals, we start to go off track. The results may not show right away, but they always show.

We don't need to be strong in every stage of our New Media Machine right away, and our Assistant will need time and patience to get up to full speed. This is all perfectly natural.

Our New Media Machine is a set of simple systems executed consistently over time. We don't need to over-complicate it, just get started and add one system at a time.

# Building a New Media Machine

So, with all the responsibility we take on as thought leaders, how do we build a New Media Machine while still running our business?

One step at a time.

Start with one system. Podcast interviews are the easiest place to start. Find a New Media Assistant who can pitch us consistently. When we get featured on podcast interviews consistently, we are gaining clarity and sharpening our Clear & Compelling Idea.

Then we launch our podcast. Once we hit on our Clear & Compelling Idea, it's time to start leading our Audience. We show up and hit record, and our Assistant runs the podcast behind the scenes.

Next, we build one great social platform. This is our online place for connection, conversation, and community. Find what works for our Audience, then our Assistant runs the system that pulls micro-content from our podcast interviews and episodes.

Finally, we create sales micro-content. Our Assistant helps pull out key pieces of content and builds it into all of our sales materials, follow up sequences, proposals, pitch decks and more.

Once those systems are running, we simply double down on what's working.

When we move forward one step at a time...

We know where to start and how to move forward—a clear vision of the road ahead allows us to move forward with no hesitation.

We find the right allies—no more wasting money hiring the wrong people or giving them the wrong work.

We build a razor-sharp Clear & Compelling Idea—a powerful idea that cannot be ignored helps grow our business easier, faster, and smoother.

We close sales faster and with less effort—better prospects come into our sales system and our micro-content helps turn them into clients we love.

Installing a New Media Machine in our business changes the conversation. Armed with a different strategy backed by a different system, can move forward with confidence. One step at a time, we choose tomorrow over today, knowing that slow and steady wins.

# Lead People to Results

People are starving for leadership.

They want to follow a leader with strong beliefs and a destination. A leader who's on a mission to solve a problem and make an impact in the world. A leader who is famously influential.

Like-minded people resonate with our mission because they feel the pain of their problem and want the results on the other side of solving it.

At the most basic level, that's why people look to thought leaders; they want to be led to new results—results they can't get on their own.

In fact, as the freelance world explodes over the next few decades, I believe thought leaders are the new "managers" in the economy. I believe this strongly, because even while the economy is changing exponentially, human nature is not.

**People still want to be led.**

People are out there right now looking for someone to lead them to new beliefs, new actions, and new results. They are looking for leaders with a Clear & Compelling Idea and a positive and polarizing Point of View, who will set a destination and invite them to come along.

Our New Media Machine puts our Clear & Compelling Idea into the world, sharing our solution to a real problem, attracting attention, and making us MicroFamous—systematically.

Once we draw in the people who resonate with our Idea, our New Media Machine shares content that cultivates new beliefs and creates ideal clients.

At that point, we can offer them opportunities to work together to solve their problem. We can also share other services, programs, or products to help them get better results. Because these other offers are consistent with our Point of View, it all makes perfect sense to our Audience. Everything we do, say, and sell comes from one Point of View and one belief system.

What does it mean to be a true leader versus just a coach or consultant?

**Here are the earmarks of a MicroFamous thought leader:**

*We sacrifice smaller problems*—so we can focus on solving one problem that delivers maximum impact.

*We care deeply about results*—if our clients don't the results we promise, we go back to the drawing board and look for solutions.

*We know our Audience*—the people we want to teach, train and lead.

*We deliver a Clear & Compelling Idea*—an idea that speaks deeply to our Audience and causes them to take action.

*We are crystal clear on the destination*—we don't just help people get further on their journey, we set the vision of where we are leading our Audience.

*We'd rather lead*—better to be first in our own niche than be a fast follower in someone else's.

When our goal is to become MicroFamous, we focus more on leadership than attention.

As we become better leaders, the content we publish becomes even more effective. Leadership is like a force-multiplier, making everything in our business more productive and effective.

We can speak to our Audience, lead them to new beliefs, new actions, and new results. We lead them from having a real problem in their business and life to seeing the results on the other side of solving that problem.

We teach, train, and lead our Audience, attracting an audience and building influence, while our New Media Machine delivers the right content to the right people.

That's why this book isn't theoretical. It's a handbook for action. A guide to becoming famously influential to the right people.

So we can build a simple, profitable business without being glued to our phone. We can move forward at our own pace. Methodical. Systematic. Relentless.

We can stop focusing on attracting attention and start focusing on leadership. We can teach, train and lead our Audience to results they can't get on their own.

Because the world doesn't need more influencers. The world needs more leaders.

# Glossary

**Battle for Attention:** The fight to break through the noise of new media content in order to attract the attention of our ideal clients and capture a leadership position.

**New Media Machine:** Content creation and promotion system that leverages the four most effective types of new media to consistently deliver a Clear & Compelling Idea, build real influence and attract ideal clients to the point where the expert wins the Battle for Attention and becomes the leader in a target niche. It's our ultimate weapon in the Battle for Attention.

**MicroFamous:** A state of being famously influential to the right people.

**Clear & Compelling Idea:** An idea at the heart of our business, which is not only compelling, but also razor-sharp clear to our audience. When an audience of ideal clients hears our Clear & Compelling Idea, they can't UN-hear it. They must take action to learn more.

**Point of View:** Our belief system, including the Buying Beliefs and our Clear & Compelling Idea

**Ideal Client:** A client we love long after we've taken their payment.

**Shrink the Battlefield:** Choose a niche we can OWN, where we become linked to solving a real problem for a particular group of like-minded people.

**Home Base:** A leadership position we've built with a specific group of like-minded people *within* our target niche. These people make up a slice of the niche that's small enough to be captured but valuable enough to generate a sustainable profit.

**Freedom of Movement:** Mapping out a flexible new media strategy that allows us to shift direction, to narrow or expand our business, without being locked into strategic decisions forever.

**Podcast Interview:** A guest appearance where we are featured on a podcast, and introduced to the audience as a trusted expert. The first stage of our New Media Machine, podcast interviews allow us to leverage outside audiences, build authority, stay consistently visible, and create new relationships with fellow thought leaders.

**Podcast:** A type of new media "show", and the second stage of our New Media Machine. Typically a podcast consists of audio episodes ranging from 10-60 minutes that are published on a consistent schedule and syndicated to apps like Apple Podcasts and Spotify. Subscribers on those apps receive new episodes automatically on their mobile devices. Podcasts can also be broadcast or recorded on live video or YouTube and then syndicated into audio podcast format.

**Influencer Conversation:** A podcast episode that features two thought leaders sharing their perspective on a topic that reinforces our Point of View and builds credibility by association.

**Micro-Content:** Small, bite-sized chunks of new media content. Can be created from scratch, such as short videos and social media content. In a New Media Machine, most micro-content is created by pulling those bite-size chunks from long-form content like podcast episodes and interviews.

**Assistant:** In-house team member who performs the daily essentials of our New Media Machine, such as pitching us on podcasts, scheduling interviews, creating graphics, posting podcast episodes and social media content, editing audio/ video for our podcast and pulling out micro-content for sales support.

**Producer:** In-house team member who handles the higher level activities of our New Media Machine. They launch new podcasts, manage new media projects, implement changes and install new systems. They also manage relationships with affiliates, outside experts, creatives and agencies so all efforts serve the current mission.

# What's Next?

In case you want a more in-depth, step by step look at using podcasting to grow your coaching, consulting or speaking business, I put together a special training.

### *The MicroFamous Podcasting Success Kit*

Steal all our best proprietary tools to leverage podcasting, including our...

- Sales Maximization Method
- Dream Guest Formula
- Call-to-Action Templates
- Relationship Accelerator System
- Influencer Conversation Framework
- Podcast Intro, Outro & Midroll Templates

We'll also share the best tips on drop dead simple podcasting equipment, recording Success Story and Solo episodes and much more!

**Claim your copy at: getmicrofamous.com/kit**

CPSIA information can be obtained
at www.ICGtesting.com
Printed in the USA
JSHW022105040420
4996JS00005B/1334